UNLEASHING

Heaven's

BREATH

Discover the Ultimate Secret
to Releasing Signs,
Wonders, & Miracles

STEVE HANNETT

UNLEASHING

Heaven's

BREATH

Discover the Ultimate Secret
TO RELEASING SIGNS,
WONDERS, & MIRACLES

DESTINY IMAGE® PUBLISHERS, INC.
P.O. Box 310, Shippensburg, PA 17257-0310
"Promoting Inspired Lives."
This book and all other Destiny Image and Destiny Image Fiction books are available at Christian bookstores and distributors worldwide.

For more information on foreign distributors, call 717-532-3040.
Or reach us on the Internet: www.destinyimage.com

ISBN 13 TP: 978-0-7684-0449-4
ISBN 13 EBook: 978-0-7684-0450-0
ISBN HC: 978-0-7684-1449-3
ISBN LP: 978-0-7684-1448-6

For Worldwide Distribution, Printed in the U.S.A.
1 2 3 4 5 6 7 8 9 10 11 /20 19 18 17 16

DEDICATION

This book is dedicated to the one I call Abba, Father, the creator of the universe. The One who loved the world so much He sent Jesus Christ to whom I will eternally give thanks and praise forever for His mercy, grace, and love. The One who died on the cross for me and revealed His healing power when He miraculously saved my life and healed me from cancer.

This book is also dedicated to all those who desperately need God to move in their lives and desire to have a personal encounter with Jesus Christ . . . the Way, the Truth, and the Life.

ACKNOWLEDGMENTS

I thank my wife, Kate, for her tireless love, support, prayer, and editing of this work. To my three beautiful children whom I consider three treasures from Heaven. To my mom and dad for their unfailing sacrificial love and support. To Dong Jin Kim, a true disciple of Jesus Christ, for his faithfulness to the Lord to boldly share the Gospel of Jesus Christ with me, resulting not only in my salvation, but also in my healing of cancer, and for his support in ministry at large. To Abundant Grace Christian Church for their prayer, intercession, love, and support, who have blessed me more than words can describe. To the servants and partners of Jesus Reigns International for their love, support, and prayers.

Trust the Words of the One who gave His life for you.

—Steve Hannett

ENDORSEMENTS

As someone who has observed the miracle working power of God, in both my Dad's (R.W. Schambach) and my own evangelistic ministries, I am always excited to read accounts in which Jesus shows Himself alive. How wonderful it has been to read about Pastor Steve Hannett's miracle healing from cancer! More importantly, I was excited to discover that Pastor Steve had not just a new insight into a Bible verse or two, he actually had a revelation of the Living Christ, as He truly IS. That revelation of Jesus and His Word has caused a powerful and effective miracle ministry to emerge in Pastor Steve's life, and he is seeing God perform mighty signs and wonders everywhere he presents Christ, around the globe.

This is the heart of *Unleashing Heaven's Breath*: knowing Jesus as He truly IS, and making Him known as He truly IS. I believe you will have an immediate faith lift upon reading this wonderful account; and, I also believe you will keep it handy as a regular resource when you watch Jesus, in an increasing measure, do mighty works through your own personal ministry.

Donna Schambach, Revivalist
SCHAMBACH MINISTRIES
www.schambach.org

Unleashing Heaven's Breath is a powerful read. This book goes beyond a simple understanding of the Bible. It is a powerful delivery of how to enter in and experience the super-natural, miraculous power of God in your life through sound biblical truth.

Darryl & Tracy Strawberry
Former Major League Baseball right fielder, ordained
Christian minister, and author
www.strawberryministries.org

Unleashing Heaven's Breath reads like a breath of fresh air from above. The truths discussed have been thought through and carefully researched. Steve Hannett the pastor, teacher, and inspiring communicator, has written what he's personally tested and proved on the mission field. He is also a trusted friend whom I've had the privilege of ministering with, and I can personally tell you that he believes and practices what he's written here.

When it comes to God's word, Steve does an excellent job of illustrating the truth that, it is not the intellectual prowess of knowledge acquired, but the humility of having knowledge revealed that sets genuine biblical Christianity apart from all belief systems on the earth.

Thinking through the issues as I read, strengthened my resolve to follow Jesus more closely in saying and doing only what I hear and see the Father saying and doing. *Unleashing Heaven's Breath* will inspire readers to relate more intimately with Jesus, allowing His Word to reside ever deeper within them.

John S. Picarello
Petra-Notes International
www.petranotes.org

We live a world where people are hungry for the supernatural and where the church is void with practical answers on how the power of God can transform a life, a community and nation? In Steve Hannett's book *Unleashing Heaven's Breath,* he teaches us how to receive and experience and demonstrate *Unleashing Heaven's Breath* which is God's Word becoming incarnate in the believer's life. The book helps believers to look intrinsically inside of their own life and discover what is blocking a release of God's power in their own life. The book in every chapter is asking the believer to walk out and be taught by the Holy Spirit by providing questions and summarizing the key points. Also, it gives us the keys of how to release His power to a lost and dying world. As I've known the author now for eight years, I have seen a great testimony *Unleashing Heaven's Breath* walked out in transformation in his personal life, his church, and to the nations he travels. I highly recommend this book.

Prophet James Jorgensen
Breath of Life Missions
www.breathoflifemissions.org

Pastor Steve Hannett's book, *Unleashing Heaven's Breath,* will take you deeper in your relationship with the LORD. I have known Pastor Steve for several years, and I am honored to write an endorsement for this book. Pastor Steve has an intense fire, hunger and passion for Jesus Christ (The Word of God). He also has the same intense desire to see God›s people walk in ALL that JESUS paid the ultimate price for all believers to have. Pastor Steve›s anointed teaching is simple to grasp, and as you apply the truths contained within the chapters of this book, you will see the impossible become possible in your day-to-day living. This book is a «must have» for every believer›s library, and is an excellent resource for Bible Study groups as well. Great ready to receive fresh revelation and impartation from the LORD, and get ready to live a supernatural lifestyle!

Lisa Buldo
Victorious Life Mentor
Author, Speaker and TV Host
Founder of Lisa Buldo International
www.LisaBuldo.com

Unleashing Heaven's Breath offers a practical understanding of the power of God's Word. Enormously helpful for those who have wondered why the demonstration of the Word of God and the proclamation of the Word of God have been missing from our culture. This book will encourage you to experience the presence of God through the Word of God.

Mariam Hency Varghese
OneHope
VP of Ministry Operations
www.onehope.net

With attentive revelation and meaningful biblical insight, Steve Hannett does an excellent job of describing the testimony of Jesus and the many facets of the Word of God in his new book, *Unleashing Heaven's Breath*. The information contained in this book will springboard your relationship with God to a higher level and challenge you to step out of your comfort zone and take God at His Word and believe Him for the impossible!

Steve Fedyski, COO
Pure Flix Entertainment

DISCLAIMER

This book is not intended as a substitute for the medical advice of physicians. The reader should regularly consult a physician in matters relating to his or her health, and particularly with respect to any symptoms that may require diagnosis or medical attention.

The information provided in this book is designed to provide helpful information on the subjects discussed. This book is not meant to be used, nor should it be used, to diagnose or treat any medical condition. For diagnosis or treatment of any medical problem, consult your own physician. The publisher and author are not responsible for any specific health or allergy needs that may require medical supervision, and are not liable for any damages or negative consequences from any treatment, action, application, or preparation to any person reading or following the information in this book.

References are provided for informational purposes only, and do not constitute endorsement of any websites or other sources. Various names and identifying details have been changed to protect the privacy of individuals. All emphasis within Scripture quotations is the author's own. Readers should be aware that the websites listed in this book may change.

CONTENTS

FOREWORD

*U*nleashing Heaven's Breath is a delightful, distinctive book that enables the reader to understand the importance and purpose of the Word of God!

As an experienced pastor, teacher and full-time church minister for more than a decade, Steve Hannett has witnessed and experienced firsthand the Word of God manifesting in his own life and the lives of many others: and he has presented this truthful understanding in this life-changing book. Those who prayerfully read this book will better grasp how God desires to use His Word in their life, what it takes to become a Word-centered believer and to have victory over the toughest obstacles in life!

As I read this book, it not only built my faith, but gave me a greater hunger to meditate upon the Word and experience Jesus' power and glory! This book is simple enough for new believers to understand and profound enough to transform the lives of the most seasoned believers! This book is filled with revelatory knowledge, and a "must read" as it has the potential to revolutionize how you live the Christian life!

Steve Hannett clearly lays out critical components needed to understand the Word of God. He explains how God's Word has the power to release the same dynamite power used to create the universe, and how God has called all believers to not only speak the Word with faith - but to demonstrate the Word with supernatural power!

Jesus told His followers they can move mountains by speaking with the mouth what they believe with the heart (Mark 11:23). Steve Hannett clearly demonstrates this same supernatural POWER not only belongs to us, but is active today!

Jesus called Himself the way, the truth, and the life (John 14:6) By studying Jesus' life, the Word made flesh, we can learn how to walk by faith, have power over sickness, disease and demons, and how to experience the miraculous. Steve Hannett brings out the truth that "God's Word and God are perfectly equal. They're inseparable, united, and one."

Unleashing Heaven's Breath shows how Jesus used the spoken Word to resist the attacks and temptations of the devil (Luke 4), and how to release that very same power in your own life. In addition, you will learn how to manifest the signs and wonders that confirm the Word of God so you may serve as a true witness of Jesus' resurrection. (Mark 16:17-20)

Steve Hannett does a magnificent job of explaining that how we receive Jesus and His Word directly determines the level of POWER that will be released from Him! He also examines in detail the Parable of the Sower and teaches the importance of properly receiving and nurturing the Word of God in our lives.

I thank God that Steve Hannett has compiled these vital revelations about God's Word in *Unleashing Heaven's Breath* for us in one book! It is truly a profound work and essential to all who want to understand how to live a fruitful live for the glory of God!

-Dr. Joseph Mattera, Mattera Ministries International

INTRODUCTION

BREATH OF GOD

All Scripture is breathed out by God . . . (2 Tim. 3:16, ESV).

Above all things, God is revealed as a supernatural Father. He's the author of creation, the God of the impossible, and the One whose heart beats with a desire to save lost sons and daughters. His love is radical, His ways amazing, and His pursuit of us relentless.

Though God has revealed Himself to mankind through dreams, visions, and angelic encounters, there remains one chosen method above all others: His Word. Throughout the ages, the Word of God has revealed not only who He is and what He desires, but also how to make His promises a reality!

The Bible is more than a book. It's more than information. It's the revelation of Jesus Christ. It is the tree of life, the portal of Heaven, and the source that will release supernatural power in your life! Every word, every chapter, and every prophecy of Scripture reveals the testimony of Jesus (see Rev. 19:10). The testimony that proves the Father's heart is to save, heal, and do the miraculous in the earth. God wants you healed! He wants you free! He wants you to receive all He has given you through the suffering and resurrection power of His Son, Jesus Christ!

You've seen and heard about others operating in the supernatural power of God. You've read books, watched movies, and seen television shows all aimed at showing us the great things God has done through others. Now it's time for your personal encounter with God's Word destined to release His supernatural power in your life. It's your turn to live and operate in the same powerful anointing of God that will bring great glory to God through His Son, Jesus Christ. It's your turn to live the kind of life that others will ask you about Jesus.

Get ready to have man-made views of the Bible broken and replaced with revelation from Heaven. Get ready to see the Word of God like you've never seen it before. Get ready for a monumental life change. Get ready for authentic, supernatural power to be released because nothing can hold back the power of God. Get ready to dig in and dive deep. Get ready to receive the life Jesus Christ died to give. It is life that flows from God's Word, God's Breath . . . Unleashing Heaven's Breath!

WHY UNLEASHING HEAVEN'S BREATH

In my distress I called upon the Lord, And cried out to my God; He heard my voice from His temple, And my cry came before Him, even to His ears. (Ps. 18:6)

Unleashing Heaven's Breath aims to unleash the power of God's Word in a practical and easy-to-understand way. Too many Bibles go unread because people never get the opportunity to spiritually understand the true nature of God's Word. Although many wonderful scholarly resources exist, they often fall short of answering our deeper heart questions such as "Can I really trust the Bible?" or "How can I understand what it teaches?" or "How can I actually receive the promises of God?"

I went to church, and heard the Name of "Jesus" my whole life. I followed what I heard, but didn't hear the Word of God. I heard the traditions of men. Thus, I had a sense of respect for God's Word, but very little understanding of it. It was during this time I was diagnosed with cancer, and during this time, I cried out to the "God out there somewhere." I literally sat in the sand on a beach looking out into the ocean sky and asked God to "teach me." As David described in Psalm 18:6, he cried out to God, and He heard his voice! God heard my cry, and the first thing He did was bring me to His Word and create an expectation that His promise would become His provision. I'll share much more detail about this amazing event, but for now, I'll say the very same day I encountered God's Word I was miraculously healed! The power of God was so intense, so real, and so life-altering I wanted to share the Gospel with everyone everywhere! Everyone needs to know the help they so desperately need is amazingly in the Bible. That black leather book so few ever read was the key to LIFE.

As a young man, I naïvely thought everyone who grew up in a Bible-believing church knew the Word of God, and must have experienced its power. Of course, they must know God's alive, and His Word is real! Then a puzzling thing happened. I began meeting sincere Christians who grew up in church, carried Bibles, and went to Bible studies and found they were shocked that I was actually healed! They never expected the things they read for so many years were actually true. They didn't understand they could receive what I had received. They had the Word, but not

His will. They had knowledge, but not understanding. They had promises, but had neither power nor provision.

Now having ministered in America for some time, I became painfully aware of the lack of clarity concerning who God is, and what His heart desires. It became clear that many years of exposure to the "religion of men" filled with the "traditions of men" had made God's Word of no effect (see Matt. 15:6). People are taught things God never said, never did, and doesn't desire. There's simply too much mixture. God knows the thoughts people think about Him, and He knows where they come from. He knows many have never heard the pure report of His Son, Jesus, and it's not only hindered their faith, but also prevented the very encounter with Him He so deeply desires for us to have.

When God revealed Himself to Moses in the midst of a burning bush in the wilderness, Moses had already spent 80 years of his life saturated with incorrect thoughts and ideas about God. In fact, Moses knew so little about the true and living God he even asked Him what His name was! God's answer is life-changing. He said, "...*I AM WHO I AM....*" (Exod. 3:14). Meditate and ponder this for a bit. God is who He is. He's the originator of all things, and can be altered by nothing and no one. The Bible boldly declares that

> *Jesus Christ is the same yesterday, today, and forever.*
> (Heb. 13:8)

While ministering at a conference in South Africa, I clearly heard Jesus tell me to be bold . . . bolder than I've ever been. The reason why really impacted me. He said, "I want people to know Me as I truly AM." It was a dramatic experience that moved me in the depths of my heart, immediately bringing me to uncontrollable tears.

God yearns for people to know Him and experience Him. He's stronger than cancer, blindness, diabetes, and every other sickness known to man. He's stronger than poverty, depression, pain, and even death! He wants people to know Him in a way that will risk all they are and all they have just to touch Him and release His power into their lives, and the lives of others! God passionately wants the world to see Him as He truly is so people from every nation under Heaven will run to Him just like the woman with the flow of blood in Mark Chapter 5!

In more than two decades of preaching, teaching, and ministering the Word of God, I've seen multitudes healed by God's Word. Many are healed in their seats at church and meetings as the Word of God is preached without laying hands on them or praying for them individually! God said in Psalm 107:20,

> *He sent His word and healed them, And delivered them*
> *from their destructions.*

It isn't necessary to touch them because they themselves touch Jesus as they are touched by His Word!

I thank God that the revelations shared in this book aren't theoretical ideas, but tried-and-true nuggets of gold that have been put through the furnace of life, and confirm the Word through accompanying signs. Whether it's been the healing of ears born deaf, tumors that have disappeared, broken legs that have straightened, limbs that have grown out before our eyes, marriages that have been restored, drug addictions that have ended, heart conditions that were reversed, and blood diseases that have disappeared, the promises of God's Word have continuously been found to be true. (See Mark 16:20.)

Too many have grown tired and discouraged hearing "about" the promises of God but failing to receive them. Too much preaching and teaching according to the traditions of the Western church has left people with little more than an expectation of "window shopping" the promises of God. This is where it's more common to hear "about" the great things God desires to do rather than to actually see people receive the great things God is doing!

It's for this reason, apart from many others, that *Unleashing Heaven's Breath* has been written. It aims to help people truly encounter Jesus Christ and to release His supernatural life and power through God's Word; it aims to produce the "testimony of the spirit of prophecy" God released through His Son (see Rev. 19:10). Above all things, God the Father desires to see the testimony of His Son come forth upon the earth. He doesn't desire to see the curse in operation, but desires to see His grace and truth in operation! The Father desires to see the finished work of His Son, Jesus, producing all it's meant to produce! Our Heavenly Father desires for us not only to know His Son, but also to have His testimony! In other words, the Father desires for us to have everything promised through His Son become our reality! It grieves the Father, Son, and Holy Spirit to see so many churches and their members living in a spiritual wilderness clinging to traditions of men rather than prospering in His grace, truth, and glory. It grieves God to see the testimony of evil advance in so many ways in so many nations. God's sons and daughters are called to release the powerful witness of the Person and Work of Jesus Christ upon the earth! It is His heart's cry, and He is calling every believer to arise to his or her calling to be filled with God's power and to release it upon the earth so all may know that Jesus Christ is the Son of God, and that there is no other way to Heaven but by Him!

Unleashing Heaven's Breath isn't meant to teach Bible study methodology, but to bridge the gap between what's read and what's lived! It's a book meant to unlock spiritual keys to enable you to spiritually commune with God's Word in a way that will release miracles, signs, and wonders in your daily life!

Remember that God's heart aches as He sees the world He came to save in turmoil and chaos! He aches to see so many living in such spiritual poverty because they neither understand nor spiritually discern what His Word is, or how to live in it. Jesus is coming back soon, and God desires to release a move upon the earth that's never been witnessed before. He desires to flood the highways and byways with His glory and the testimony of His Son's blood. It's an hour many know they need more than entertainment in church. Their hearts cry out for more because they know there's more . . . much more! They long to excel into new dimensions with God, and hunger to know Him as He truly is! It's time to no longer seek just moments of glory, but to rely upon His Word like the air we breathe. It will produce a sustained movement of God that moves across the earth like a glory-tsunami!

Unleashing Heaven's Breath seeks to produce the following blessings in your life and/or ministry:

- Enable you to more fully release the power of God's Word in your life and ministry.

- Facilitate supernatural intimacy with God's Word.

- Unlock and activate your ministry to produce miracles, signs, and wonders.

- Establish you in a lifelong, revelatory relationship with God's Word.

- Establish you in the revelation that the Word of God is supernatural, God-breathed, and Heaven-released.

- Provide you with the inspiration and understanding you need to grow exponentially in your commitment to becoming "one" with the Word of God.

- Establish you as a true witness of the testimony of the resurrected Christ in all the world to fulfill Christ's Great Commission.

UNLEASHING HEAVEN'S BREATH IS FOR YOU

Unleashing Heaven's Breath is written in a conversational manner filled with revelations, encouragements, testimonies, and questions for reflection all aimed at helping you understand the Word of God with a fresh, Heavenly perspective. It's therefore very much like a mentoring manual to gently lead you from impacting ideas to powerful life-applications.

Whether you're someone who's been a bit skeptical about the validity of the Bible or a Bible scholar fully versed in hermeneutical theory, *Unleashing Heaven's Breath* seeks to speak to the depths of your soul and "inner man." It's my prayerful expectation that whether you are a first-time seeker of Jesus or have walked with Jesus for many years, you'll have a fresh, life-changing encounter with Jesus as you come to understand deeper dimensions of God's living Word!

If you've known the Word of God as a complicated book filled with information . . . this book is for you. If you desire to really connect with God's Word in deeper ways . . . this book is for you. If you've had questions as to whether you can trust the Bible, this book is for you. If you're struggling with something in your life and desperately need God's help, this book is for you! If you want to see Jesus as He is, encounter His power, and become part of God's army who serves as a witness of the testimony of Jesus to all nations, then *Unleashing Heaven's Breath* is for you!

HOW TO GET THE MOST OUT OF *UNLEASHING HEAVEN'S BREATH*

Unleashing Heaven's Breath has been designed as a manual for life change. It seeks to build a solid foundation and serve as a paradigm transformation project concerning how the Word of God should be viewed and lived within life and ministry.

Allowing the Lord to create deep systemic change in our heart is a process. It may begin with being exposed to new information, but it ends with a deep transformation of the heart. We need to take great care to ensure long-lasting transformation takes place . . . especially concerning how we see and live with the Word of God! The following steps are recommended to help guide you in the process and to ensure the "birds of the air" (see Matt. 13:4,18–19) will never steal even one seed of God's Word from you.

READING IT THROUGH

After the first reading of *Unleashing Heaven's Breath,* it is highly recommended to read sequentially from the beginning to the end. Each chapter builds upon the other, as the revelation in one chapter is often applied in subsequent chapters. Take time to personally look up the Scripture references. Meditate on the verses, and allow the Holy Spirit to speak directly to you.

QUESTIONS FOR REFLECTION

It's recommended to go back over the chapter and review the sections the Lord impressed upon your heart. Closely review the "Questions for Reflection" and the "Chapter Summary Points." Take ample time to think through the questions as this is the critical step through which the Holy Spirit will frequently lead, guide, and speak to you concerning the issues of your heart.

JOURNALING WITH GOD

Biblical meditation is the process of prayerfully pondering the Scriptures, and journaling is the process of recording the things the Lord is showing you. It's the process by which you come to the place of articulating the revelations and convictions of your heart. It's also the place you record how you will practically apply and act on God's truth. We need to ensure we're not only hearers of God's Word, but also doers (see James 1:25).

PRAYER

Saturate yourself with prayer throughout the reading of the book so your spiritual senses are ready to receive the things God desires to impart. Talk with God about the things He's revealing and showing. Press into the exciting areas God is growing you in, and allow your faith to make firm declarations of faith to move mountains (see Matt. 21:21)!

Part I

THE PORTAL
TO
POWER

Chapter 1

TOUCHING JESUS

OUR GOOD, GOOD FATHER

The heart of God has always been to live in the most intimate of relationships with His sons and daughters—a relationship that goes far beyond what we normally understand or ever experience. When Adam and Eve, and all who followed, fell into sin separating us from God, the Father sent His Son, Jesus Christ, into the world to save us and restore us into the Father's arms. This restoration is so deep and so powerful I would venture to say we, the Body of Christ, have only begun to understand the depths of the blessings it provides. Through Jesus Christ, we can literally touch God and experience His glory and supernatural power!

I know this to be true because I'm a living witness! I grew up hearing frequently about God but never once saw His power touch anyone. I grew up in a religious tradition that taught me to expect a better life in heaven, but never created an expectation that I could experience God's power on earth. It wasn't until I was diagnosed with cancer at the age of 19 years that I really cried out to God for help and discovered that He indeed is a good, good Father.

You see, I knew what it was like to experience the side effects of radiation treatment. I knew what it was like to not be able to swallow my own saliva because of pain, and I knew what it was like to fear my uncertain future. However, because of the goodness, mercy, and unfailing compassion of God, He heard my cry, introduced me to His Son, Jesus, and literally flooded me with His power completely eradicating every cancer cell from my body.

This encounter was more than a one-time event to tell a story. It was an experience God used to teach me how I, and all who would come to Jesus, could live with His miracle-working power on a daily basis! I'll share much more detail about my story and the lessons I learned, but let's begin our journey with someone else who was desperate for a miracle.

SHE NEEDED A MIRACLE!

Now a woman, having a flow of blood for twelve years, who had spent all her livelihood on physicians and could not be healed by any, (Luke 8:43)

We don't know her name. The Gospel of Mark only introduces her as a "certain woman" (see Mark 5:25). We do know she suffered for 12 straight years with a bleeding condition that not only physically debilitated her, but, according to Jewish Levitical law, also made her spiritually unclean (see Lev. 15:19–28). Making things worse, she suffered financial problems having spent all she had on doctors, despite the fact she grew worse! We can only imagine the level of despair and discouragement she experienced for 12 years with no help or hope in sight.

Then something powerful happened. She heard about Jesus Christ of Nazareth. She didn't hear about a local church, a prayer meeting, a worship concert, an outreach event, or even a healing meeting. She didn't hear about Jewish law or religious tradition, and never attended a Bible college or even one healing seminar. She simply received pure, unadulterated revelation of the One called Yeshua (Jesus). The report she heard created a hope so powerful it pierced and overwhelmed her pain, rejection, and discouragement.

When the day came when Jesus was close enough for her to approach, she was consumed with revelation and faith! She saw the promised One! She saw the One who could make her whole! She saw the hope of her Messiah, and her fear, failure, and frustration were no match for her faith in the presence of His glory. She was so overwhelmed with excitement and expectancy she said, *". . . If only I may touch His garment, I shall be made well."* (Matt. 9:21). It didn't matter to her that Jewish law forbade her, an unclean woman, to touch a man. Her faith compelled her to press through the multitude and touch Jesus. We can imagine this frail woman using all her strength to press through the large crowd to stretch forth her hand to touch Jesus Christ, the Lamb of God slain before the foundations of the world (Rev. 13:8). Immediately, the supernatural power of God was released from Jesus and flooded her body. The power and light of Jesus Christ overwhelmed the darkness working within her body, and she was instantly healed! **Twelve years of pain ended with one faith-filled touch** (see Matt. 9:21), a touch we are meant not only to learn from, but also to experience!

THE RETURN TO TRUTH

My people are destroyed for lack of knowledge. Because you have rejected knowledge, I also will reject you from being priest for Me; Because you have forgotten

the law of your God, I also will forget your children.
(Hos. 4:6)

There's no question we both desire and need to experience the miraculous power of God like this "certain" woman. We long to overcome doubt, to press through the crowd, and to receive healing from the living, breathing Son of God. We long to drink from the limitless depth of God's rich wells of goodness, mercy, and love. We want to pack up the desert tents we've been living in and move into the promised land covenanted by God.

The wonderful "Good News" of Jesus Christ is that God also desires these blessings for us! Jesus desires for us to pull on the hem of His garment with our faith! He longs to release His power into our lives, bodies, marriages, families, and churches! It's why the Father sent Him! It's why Jesus willingly laid down His life on the cross, was buried, and rose again in victory! God doesn't want us cursed! He wants us blessed! Jesus wants to release the fullness of Himself to all who desire to touch Him!

People sometimes teach that miracles like the healing of the woman with the flow of blood were for them alone because God works in "mysterious ways," that God in His divine sovereignty desired to heal only a few, that Jesus performed supernatural miracles merely to demonstrate His divinity among the multitudes then, and that the days of miracles have ended. Others believe that God still performs miracles, but that the best they can do is hope and pray that God will somehow make the decision to touch them. They sometimes pray for years waiting for God's divine time. Sadly, many resign to believe it wasn't God's will to heal them because their "time" never seemed to come.

The premise underlying these views originates from sincere people whose faith derives more from personal experience and

religious tradition than from biblical precedent. When enough people personally experience the same thing over time, it easily becomes a "corporate truth" from which religious traditions are formed. These "religious traditions" form almost universally accepted beliefs that often go unchallenged. Thus, beliefs that the "days of miracles have ended" or that "God heals only some" or that "God will heal in His own time" go uncontested, resulting in the destruction of the faith of many! Preachers, teachers, and others who have received these errant beliefs built upon the fragility of man's experience have a great need to return to the immutable knowledge of God.

In the Book of Hosea, God reveals the priests failed to properly teach God's laws to the nation, resulting in a lack of knowledge that led to the destruction of His own people! Forgetting and neglecting God's truth has terrible consequences, and all who desire to walk in God's blessings must come out of every teaching rooted in the wisdom of man, and return to the purity of God's knowledge.

The reality of this "certain woman's" healing is very powerful because it provides a clear and undeniable example of the faith of a woman who never wondered whether God "could" heal or "would" heal or whether it was His time. No! Her faith boldly declared, *". . . If only I may touch His garment, I shall be made well."* (Matt. 9:21). She expected God to heal her, and for it to happen right then and there!

A SUPERNATURAL TOUCH

For she said, "If only I may touch His clothes, I shall be made well." (Mark 5:28)

Some think this woman was healed because she touched Jesus' physical body. In fact, I've heard people say they believe it was easier to get healed during Jesus' time on earth because He was physically present. Thank God this isn't at all true! We have just as much access to Jesus now as the woman who touched Him then! Think of it—multitudes thronged and pressed Jesus' physical body, and nothing happened to them (see Mark 5:31). No one else was healed or reported power entering them. Only the touch of this woman caused Jesus' power to be released. **This means it wasn't her "physical" touch but her "spiritual" touch that made the difference.** Despite years filled with failure to get well, her heart was fully persuaded that Jesus was so glorious that all she had to do was touch His clothes and she would be healed. Her faith received Jesus' supernatural power! Her faith declaration catapulted her into the realm of the supernatural, and enabled her to experience Jesus as He truly is . . . a supernatural, power-filled Savior.

There's no question in my mind that people would love to search for the clothes Jesus wore that day. They would build a huge monument, and people would come from afar to touch the hem of the garment, declaring the natural cloth had miracle power. Nevertheless, the truth is that Jesus' clothing had very little to do with the miracle. When Jesus asked, "Who touched Me?" He revealed someone had touched Him more deeply than His mere clothing. Someone sparked a supernatural encounter with Him. When the disciples heard Jesus' question, they were confused because they thought the multitudes thronged and pressed into Him naturally. They had no idea of the spiritual transaction that occurred in the supernatural realm. **They didn't understand that Jesus' real question wasn't who "physically" touched Him, but rather who supernaturally accessed Him.**

Thank God the true nature of the miracle wasn't due to Jesus' clothing, because we don't have them! Thank God we have what she had . . . the promise of healing, deliverance, transformation, and a new life through Jesus Christ! We can believe and receive just like this "certain" woman!

Jesus hasn't left us orphans! Jesus is as much here on the earth as He was in the Gospel era! As believers in a resurrected Savior who dwells within us, we can touch Him! We simply need to learn how to *access* Him!

GOD'S TIME IS NOW

"The Spirit of the Lord is upon Me, Because He has anointed Me To preach the gospel to the poor; He has sent Me to heal the brokenhearted, To proclaim liberty to the captives And recovery of sight to the blind, To set at liberty those who are oppressed; To proclaim the acceptable year of the Lord." (Luke 4:18–19)

Generations of Israelites waited for the Messiah. They had the prophetic promises of Yeshua, but never enjoyed the fulfillment of His actual coming. They were able to only wait in expectation that by the Messiah's stripes, they would be healed (see Isa. 53:5). We, however, have no need to wait! Jesus has come, suffered, died, and has been resurrected back to life forevermore! God's timing to save, heal, and deliver through Jesus Christ was revealed the moment Jesus Christ was conceived by the Holy Spirit in the virgin Mary! Right now, Jesus is alive and sitting at the right hand of the Father! We're no longer waiting for God to send help! God has sent His Word and healed us, and has delivered us from all our destruction (see Ps. 107:20)! We're no longer waiting for God . . . He's waiting for us!

In the Gospel of Luke, Jesus declared the fulfillment of the prophecy of Isaiah that the Savior had arrived and the Spirit of the Lord was upon Him to preach the Good News to the poor, to heal the brokenhearted, to proclaim liberty to the captives, to bring sight to the blind, to set the oppressed free, and to declare the acceptable year of the Lord. The "acceptable year of the Lord" referred to the year of Jubilee, which simply meant the time for liberation and joy had come!

Let's return to the account of the woman with the flow of blood in the Gospel of Mark to see this truth in action!

When she heard about Jesus, she came behind Him in the crowd and touched His garment. For she said, "If only I may touch His clothes, I shall be made well." (Mark 5:27–28)

In this account, Jesus didn't initiate this healing miracle. It was initiated by the woman in need. Jesus didn't touch the woman; she touched Him! In fact, Jesus wasn't even paying any noticeable attention to her as He was on His way to heal a centurion's daughter. Jesus simply recognized that someone touched Him and caused power to be transferred from Him to her! Her touch stopped God right in His tracks because He knew someone accessed that which was inside of Him! Think of it! An ordinary, suffering, feeble, spiritually unclean woman initiated this supernatural transaction with God!

What is even more amazing is that she never even asked Jesus to heal her! There's no supplication, no plea, no request, no petition, no fasting, and no presentation to God explaining how long or how much she suffered. No humble speech such as "Lord, if it be thy will, please heal me" as seen in other references like Matthew 8:2. She simply touched Jesus with the faith declaration that she would be healed, and she was. She accessed the covenanted promise of healing provided by God's Word released in and through Jesus Christ. She accessed the Alpha and the Omega! The result was her instantaneous, supernatural healing! In fact, Jesus more fully revealed that it wasn't because of an incidental decision to heal her, but rather because she was able to access Him through faith. Jesus didn't say He had decided to make her well, but said, "*. . . Daughter, your faith has made you well. Go in peace, and be healed of your affliction.*" (Mark 5:34).

Of course, we know the woman never "made" God do anything. No human being can ever dictate to God. It's not that this woman "took" something from Jesus, but rather that she received who was given to her by her Father. The Gospel of John declares that with Moses came the law, but with Jesus "came" both grace and truth. She simply accessed and received the grace and truth sent to her (see John 1:17)! If the grace of God hadn't already been extended to her, she never would've even been able to get close to Jesus!

If she believed she needed to wait for God to make a decision to heal her, she never would have believed with such certainty. Her faith in who He was, and what He had to give, compelled her to touch Him. Jewish religious tradition would have cautioned the woman to stay away, but she couldn't. Modern religious tradition cautions us not to think so boldly, but we must! God had made the decision to open the Heavens to us when He sent Jesus Christ, and God Himself is now waiting for us to press through the crowd and receive His Word, Jesus Christ, the One who heals us and delivers us from all our destructions.

GOD'S CALL TO ALL

The woman with the flow of blood wasn't the beneficiary of a one-time miracle, but was rather an example to all who would desire to access the supernatural power of God through Jesus Christ! When most people are passively waiting for God to "move" on them or to "touch" them, the Word of God is teaching that we can go to Him and touch Him! As James 4:8 says, *"Draw near to God and He will draw near to you. . . ."* Jesus declared in the Gospel of Luke,

> *"The Spirit of the Lord is upon Me, Because He has anointed Me To preach the gospel to the poor; He has sent Me to heal the brokenhearted, To proclaim liberty to the captives And recovery of sight to the blind, To set at liberty those who are oppressed; To proclaim the acceptable year of the Lord."* (Luke 4:18–19)

Jesus declared it was time for freedom and Jubilee (see Luke 4:18)! All could be free and receive the emancipation proclaimed in the Good News! All who believe, receive, and act on God's provision can gladly expect all that has been promised in Jesus Christ to come true!

God isn't asking us to make the first move, but to respond to His move of sending Jesus Christ into the world for us (see James 4:8)! He boldly invites the sinner, the sick, and the burdened to come to Him (see Matt. 11:28–30)!

I believe Jesus knew this woman would come to Him. I believe He longed for her desperation to make contact with His love. I believe Jesus was filled with joy when her "faith" touched Him. I believe He couldn't wait to tell the whole world someone accessed His power. I believe that right now Jesus longs for the day we would see past a mere story and discover the divine blueprint for understanding how we can access the supernatural grace and power within Him—a blueprint that enables transformation at the deepest of levels, a blueprint repeatedly found throughout the pages of the book we call the Bible.

Too many have spent all they have on failed treatments. Too many have been living in the bondage of sickness, disease, and other works of darkness! Too few have touched Jesus in the way that causes power to flow from Him! Too few access the supernatural power of God in their lives.

Don't fret, worry, or become discouraged anymore! No condition, no situation, and no track record of failure is beyond the reach of God's power and love! Remove your focus away from the difficult circumstance of "here" and "now," and lay hold of the powerful faith-confession that declared, *". . . If only I may touch His garment, I shall be made well."* (Matt. 9:21). Today, wherever you are and whatever you or a loved one may be going through, make the heart decision to press through and "touch" Jesus. Have confidence that if this "certain" woman was allowed, by grace, to touch Jesus and walk in His supernatural power, so can you.

Get ready! It's time to dig deeper and unveil the true nature of God's Word. It's time to discover what she really touched when she touched Jesus in the supernatural realm. It's time for you to unleash God's supernatural power in your own life!

CHAPTER SUMMARY POINTS

1. The miracle that this woman experienced began with hearing a pure report of Jesus Christ. She received a pure, unadulterated revelation of the One called Yeshua. The revelation of Jesus Christ created a clear expectation of unwavering faith that released her healing. We need to receive such a report

from God's Word, and become liberated from all things that aren't from our Heavenly Father.

2. Personal experience and religious tradition should never be the foundation of our faith and expectation. We need to return to the Word of God to develop a pure report of Jesus. Only by receiving God's knowledge can we receive faith-building expectation of God's supernatural blessings.

3. The woman's healing didn't result from a natural touch, but resulted from a supernatural faith-touch. It's not the flesh that brings life, but rather the Spirit (see John 6:63).

4. As believers, we shouldn't be waiting for God to decide "if" He's going to heal or "who" He's going to heal. When God sent His Son, Jesus, to the earth, He sent Him so all may receive Him and all may become blessed through Him. The sending of Jesus Christ into the world is the revelation of God's decision to save, heal, and deliver all people all the time!

5. Jesus Christ is calling all believers to come boldly to His throne of grace and to access Him! Too many are waiting for God to move when God is waiting for His people to come and touch Him! Jesus has been given to us that we may freely receive from Him (see Heb. 4:16)! Don't allow human tradition to keep you from boldly receiving the love and supernatural power of God!

6. The miracle of this "certain" woman was never meant to be an isolated incident. God desires for us to learn from her, and to follow in her footsteps. God desires for us to believe Him in such a way that we'll come to Him and expect the promises of God to be "Yes" and "Amen" (see 2 Cor. 1:20).

7. God is calling *all* to come. No sin, problem, or difficulty is greater than God's grace! Jesus can be received by all who come with a humble heart (see James 4:6).

8. It's time to prepare our hearts to come to a fuller understanding of the Word of God and what the woman really touched when she touched Jesus in the supernatural realm.

QUESTIONS FOR REFLECTION

1. What things have I heard about Jesus? Have they come from God's Word, or have they come from sincere people who have mixed information about Jesus?

2. Has what I received about Jesus caused the kind of faith to well up in me like the woman with the flow of blood? Why or why not?

3. What things in my life do I need to press through to touch Jesus with faith?

4. Have I been waiting for God to send help He has already sent? Do I believe I can go with confidence to both access and receive the finished work of Jesus Christ?

5. Do I believe I can walk in the supernatural power of God as a lifestyle for all the world to see?

PRAYER

Father, I thank You that You've already made the decision to send Your only begotten Son, Jesus Christ, for me. Lord, I pray that I fully receive all that has been sent to me in Jesus.

Abba, I pray that I would encounter Your Son Jesus in the way that causes Your power to flow within me! I desire to walk in Your supernatural power, and decree that I will abide in You and Your Word like never before. Teach me and lead me into a fuller revelation of Your Word and what the woman with the flow of blood really touched!

Lord, I declare that my best days are yet to come for Your glory. Thank You, Jesus!

Chapter 2

THE BREATH OF HEAVEN

OUR GREAT NEED

The thief does not come except to steal, and to kill, and to destroy. I have come that they may have life, and that they may have it more abundantly. (John 10:10)

All across the world, there are people in the greatest of need. Whether it be hunger, sickness, war, abuse, poverty, and the like, evil is working upon the earth to kill, steal, and destroy. Although God has already sent His Son, Jesus Christ, into the world and a countless number of churches exist, suffering seems to persist at an ever-growing rate. This isn't at all because God desires it, but because so many never learned how to touch or be touched by God.

Even further, although the Name of Jesus Christ is probably the most well-known Name in all the earth, it's arguably the least understood. Some say Jesus was just a good moral teacher, others say He was just a prophet, and still others say He's the resurrected Son of God who rescues us from the curse of sin and death. One only needs to visit a few Christian denominations to get the urge to ask, "Will the real Jesus please stand?"

If we want to experience the supernatural power of Jesus Christ like the woman with the flow of blood, we need to encounter more than religious philosophy and the traditions of men. We need revelation and understanding of how to "touch" and "be touched" by the miracle power of God. We need to encounter Jesus Christ Himself! **Specifically, we need three things: an understanding of the source of supernatural power, an understanding of how to access it, and an understanding of how to live by it.**

REVELATORY VERSUS SENSORY KNOWLEDGE

Our Western, scientific culture has trained us well in the study of the natural world. Though often unaware of it, we apply the Scientific Method to things we learn daily. The *Oxford English Dictionary* defines it as "the method or procedure that has characterized natural science since the seventeenth century, consisting in systematic observation, measurement and experiment, and the formulation, testing, and modification of hypotheses".[1] Put another way, we want to see, test, and judge everything according to our five senses (sensory knowledge), which include sight (ophthalmoception), hearing (audioception), taste (gustaoception), smell (olfacoception), and touch (tactioception). We've been molded to trust the things we can see, manage, and measure and to distrust the things that are unseen, unmanageable, and unmeasurable. This has caused us to unconsciously harbor adverse thoughts and feelings in relation to the things of the supernatural, leading us to become dangerously unaware of it in our daily lives.

The Word of God clearly teaches not only that we need to be aware of the spiritual world, but also that there's a critical and important relationship that exists between the spiritual and the physical world. It reveals that our physical world—the things we can see, manage, and measure—has actually been created by the things in the spiritual world, which we can't see, manage, or measure!

> *By faith we understand that the worlds were framed by the word of God, so that the things which are seen were not made of things which are visible.* (Heb. 11:3)

In addition, the apostle Paul wrote to the Corinthian church exhorting them not to look at what is seen, but rather to look at what isn't seen because that which is unseen is more important!

> *Therefore we do not lose heart. Even though our outward man is perishing, yet the inward man is being renewed day by day. For our light affliction, which is but for a moment, is working for us a far more exceeding and eternal weight of glory, while we do not look at the things which are seen, but at the things which are not seen. For the things which are seen are temporary, but the things which are not seen are eternal.* (2 Cor. 4:16–18)

The great deception working in the minds of many sincere believers is that the supernatural realm is either nonexistent or nonessential. This has caused many to trust exclusively in sensory knowledge, bringing great detriment to their Christian walk.

Revelatory knowledge is understanding that can't be grasped through intellectual study. It's understanding that goes beyond intellectual ability because it comes from that which is specially "revealed," or made known by God. A person can study for years and never come close to the depth of understanding that comes from one revelatory moment with God. Revelation pierces the mind and soul, and brings both clarity and certainty to spiritual matters. Living by sensory knowledge alone will cause you to become trapped by the depravity of human reasoning, whereas living by revelatory knowledge will elevate you into the glory realm of God's mind. God says,

> *"For My thoughts are not your thoughts, Nor are your ways My ways," says the Lord. "For as the heavens are higher than the earth, So are My ways higher than your ways, And My thoughts than your thoughts."* (Isa. 55:8–9)

No one can ever live a successful Christian life by walking in the limitations of human reasoning. The Bible even tells us that our carnal minds are even hostile toward the things of God and that those who live according to their natural natures can't please God!

> *For those who live according to the flesh set their minds on the things of the flesh, but those who live according to the Spirit, the things of the Spirit. For to be carnally minded is death, but to be spiritually minded is life and peace. Because the carnal mind is enmity against God; for it is not subject to the law of God, nor indeed can be. So then, those who are in the flesh cannot please God.* (Rom. 8:5–8)

The successful supernatural life depends on receiving and living by the knowledge revealed by the Word of God. The foundation of a life lived in the supernatural power of God must be lived not by the senses, but by the revelation of God. In addition, the spiritual world is so far above the natural world that it's impossible to learn it or understand it with our natural minds. Paul explicitly shared this with the Corinthians in these words:

> *But the natural man does not receive the things of the Spirit of God, for they are foolishness to him; nor can he know them, because they are spiritually discerned. But he who is spiritual judges all things, yet he himself is rightly judged by no one. For "who has known the mind of the Lord that he may instruct Him?" But we have the mind of Christ.* (1 Cor. 2:14–16)

Truly, if God's Word isn't spiritually discerned, it cannot be spiritually understood. Thus, God supernaturally reveals His knowledge to us. The apostle Paul says,

> *But as it is written: "Eye has not seen, nor ear heard, Nor have entered into the heart of man The things which God has prepared for those who love Him." But God has revealed them to us through His Spirit. For the Spirit searches all things, yes, the deep things of God. For what man knows the things of a man except the spirit of the man which is in him? Even so no one knows the things of God except the Spirit of God.* (1 Cor. 2:9–11)

Some may think the woman with the flow of blood merely touched the hem of Jesus' garment naturally, but her faith propelled her from the physical realm into the spiritual realm. She moved with revelatory knowledge, enabling her to access the "unseen" Word of God in the spiritual realm, resulting in her visible, physical healing according to the principle of creation found in Hebrews 11:3. That which was unseen created her miracle that was able to be seen! Her faith was *". . . the substance of things hoped for, the evidence of things not seen."* (Heb. 11:1).

MORE THAN MEETS THE EYE

Now after six days Jesus took Peter, James, and John his brother, led them up on a high mountain by themselves; and He was transfigured before them. His face shone like the sun, and His clothes became as white as the light. (Matt. 17:1–2)

Many people "see" the Word of God as the "big black book" that many confess to be . . . well . . . I'll say it . . . boring and nearly impossible to understand. They've been taught to honor and respect it, but often find it hard to muster up the motivation to read it. The sad truth is that even sincere Christians are being caught up in the cultural wave of our time that views the Bible as an irrelevant book written by men. Said another way, people have come to "see" the Bible through a natural, rather than a spiritual, lens, and judge it according to its outward appearance rather than its inward revelation. As many saw the incarnate Jesus no deeper than His flesh, worn clothing, and homeless condition, so people today see the Bible no deeper than a black leather, gilded-edged book with hard-to-pronounce words. Nevertheless, God desires for us to see beyond the natural and to behold the true nature of His Word. His gentle but powerful voice declares in the hearts of the seeking that the Bible is more than meets the natural eye.

One day, Jesus took Peter, James, and John, his brother, up on a high mountain by themselves, and Jesus became transfigured before them. His face began to shine bright like the sun, and His clothing became as white as the light (see Matt. 17:1–2)! Jesus, in an intimate place, decided to open the spiritual eyes of the disciples so they may receive the revelation of His true identity. It's as if Jesus peeled back His natural appearance so His closest friends could understand that He is more than meets the eye. He is truly supernatural!

In the midst of a bright, glory cloud that overshadowed them, a voice broke out declaring that Jesus was God's Son in whom the Father was well pleased and that the disciples should "Hear Him!" (see Matt. 17:5). Not only did Jesus Christ, the Son of God, unveil His true nature, but also God, the Father, affirmed it while issuing the command to "Hear Him!" God was saying, "now that you've seen My Son is supernatural, **I want you to hear and come under His supernatural Word! I want you to relate to Him with your new revelation that He's more than just a man! He's more than what others perceive Him to be! He's My Son, and He fully represents Me! My Word and His Word are One. He's the revelation of My Word, so Hear Him!"**

I believe Peter, James, and John went down that mountain understanding with fearful clarity that Jesus was much more than He naturally appeared to be to the masses. They never saw the "big black book" we call the Bible, but they beheld the supernatural, radiant glory of God in Jesus and received God's command to hear and follow His Word! Without question, God desires to peel back the black leather cover and unveil the truly supernatural nature of His Word to us today!

THE BREATH OF HIS MOUTH

By the word of the Lord the heavens were made, And all the host of them by the breath of His mouth. (Ps. 33:6)

God's omnipresent! He's everywhere! At this very moment He's present in the celestial realm of Heaven, the realm of space containing an innumerable number of stars, and He's present in the realm called earth. There's no place in existence that God isn't! He's almighty, and above every power. He has no weakness, and nothing is able to contend or compete with Him. He's supreme in every way. All creation bows to Him and operates under His sovereign authority. He's timeless, and has no beginning or end. His glory is from everlasting to everlasting (see Ps. 90:2) and limitless in power. He isn't just mighty, but might itself. He isn't just powerful, but power itself! He isn't just filled with light, but is light itself (see 1 John 1:5)! He isn't just filled with love, but is love itself (see 1 John 4:8)!

Moreover, this amazing, indescribable, uncontested, all-powerful God numbers the stars and knows each one by name (see Ps. 147:4)! He even knows your name, and the number of hairs upon your head (see Matt. 10:30). Power knows your name! Light knows your name! Love knows your name, and He's radically passionate for you! You're the apple of His eye (see Zech. 2:8), His beloved (see Song of Sol. 2:16), and He longs for your well-being and to be one with you!

In fact, His love for His lost sons and daughters was so intense He could no longer send ambassador prophets, messengers, and judges. They all walked in the frailty of their sinful Adamic nature and were unable to bring the fullness of the restoration God desired. God desired to send the fullness of His heart, the fullness of His compassion, and the fullness of His power so He could heal us and deliver us from all our destructions.

How did God do it? **How did He release the fullness of His power, authority, sovereignty, and love upon the earth? What**

could God send to contain the glory, power, and fullness of Himself? What could be so united with the fullness of Himself that it would be equal with Himself and His very righteousness? What could possibly be equal with God? He could only send but one thing . . . His very own Word.

You see, God's Word and God are perfectly equal. They're inseparable, united, and one. God's Word emanates from His very being. It's not something that describes God, but something that is God. When God speaks, He releases Himself. Simply put, God's Word releases God. Whenever God speaks, He releases whatever is in Him. The Bible reveals that

> *By the word of the Lord the heavens were made, And all the host of them by the breath of His mouth.* (Ps. 33:6)

When God speaks His Word, He releases His breath, and when He releases His breath, He releases His very life within Him. This is Unleashing Heaven's Breath! It's the release of God's Word of life from His mouth!

God is light (see 1 John 1:5), and God said, "Let there be light," so light came into being (see Gen. 1:1–3)! What God had, God released through His Word! Even the God-life that filled mankind during His creation finds its source from the breath of God!

> *And the Lord God formed man of the dust of the ground, and breathed into his nostrils the breath of life; and man became a living being.* (Gen. 2:7)

When God saw the destruction of sin and death upon the earth and desired to save us, He sent His Word to heal and deliver us from all our destructions! Yes, people today see a black leather book, but this really isn't the spiritual reflection of God's Word at all. When we think of God's Word like this, we'll fall into the paradigm of earthly thinking rather than Heavenly understanding.

I once received a phone call from a new believer asking me to answer a question someone asked her about the Bible. The question went something like this: "How can people trust the Bible when so many translations exist?" It's a good question I gladly spent time helping her understand. I briefly shared how the different translations came to be, about the early writings we have, and about the interpretive origins of Greek, Hebrew, and Aramaic as these topics are important and vital to properly work through the issue. Later, however, upon deeper reflection, I laughed within myself, asking another question. When God said, "Let there be light" in Genesis 1:3, what language did He speak? Hebrew, Greek, Aramaic, Latin, English, Spanish, German, Portuguese, Chinese, Tagalu, Bahasa, Russian, Swahili? Did He speak in the King James English, New American Standard Bible translation, maybe the Amplified or English Standard Version? Of course not! Human language wasn't even created yet! No one knows the original sound of God's Word, but we know it transcends everything we could imagine! God's Word and the Heavenly sound it released pierced the cosmos with His majesty and glory! It's not limited by human capacity, the sound spectrum of the human ear, or anything else! It's one with God, and it's above all things! It's supracultural, and it's absolutely supernatural!

When God the Father revealed His Word to Moses on Mount Sinai and to Peter, James, and John on the Mount of Transfiguration, He revealed more than simply information about God. He revealed Himself. In Hebrew, He released His *Ruach*, or Heavenly wind, Spirit, or breath (Strong's Hebrew #7307).

When the early disciples were gathered in the evening of the first day of the week, they were afraid of the Jews, and the doors were shut as they were in hiding. Then Jesus appeared and said, "Peace be with you." Then, after He showed them His hands and His side, the disciples knew it was Jesus and were so happy to see Him. Jesus once again spoke and said, "Peace to you! As the Father has sent Me, I also send you." Then Jesus did something amazing. From the depth of His eternal, resurrected, glorified body, He *breathed* upon them, and said, "Receive the Holy Spirit." Truly, God's breath transcends any earthly language, and is the true release of God's power and authority upon earth. It's the unquestionable, undeniable vehicle that He's chosen not only to create all things, but also to release His grace and truth in the earth.

Chapter Summary Points

1. If we want to experience the supernatural power of Jesus Christ like the woman with the flow of blood, we need to encounter more than religious philosophy and the traditions of men. We need revelation and understanding of how to "touch" and "be touched" by the supernatural power of God. We need to encounter Jesus Christ Himself! **Specifically, we need three things:** an understanding of the source of supernatural power, an understanding of how to access it, and an understanding of how to live by it.

2. We have been well conditioned to rely upon our natural five senses, but God desires for His children to live according to revelatory knowledge in His Word. He desires to reveal His mind so we may live according to His covenanted promises and not according to human reason.

3. Just as Jesus revealed to the disciples closest to Him that He was more than His natural flesh on the Mount of Transfiguration, so God wants to reveal that His Word is more than simply a book filled with information. God's Word is eternal, Heavenly, and supernatural.

4. The only thing God could send to earth that was truly equal to Himself was His Word. God's Word transcends all human language, and when God speaks His Word, He releases His breath and His very life within Him. This is Unleashing Heaven's Breath! It's the release of God's Word of life from His mouth!

QUESTIONS FOR REFLECTION

1. In what ways has your Christian walk been influenced by the traditions of men? In what ways has your Christian walk been influenced by true encounters with God's Spirit?

2. Think about the two types of knowledge: sensory and revelatory. In what areas has your faith been guided by sensory knowledge, and in what areas has your faith been guided by revelatory knowledge?

3. What have been your traditional views about the Bible? In what ways do you think Peter, James, and John thought differently about Jesus Christ after His transfiguration? What changes took place concerning how they would hear and follow Jesus? What changes do you think would take place concerning how you would listen and follow the Word of God if you had the same revelation that the Bible was also God's Word?

4. How would your view of God's Word change if you came to understand that His Word truly originated from the breath

of His mouth rather than the will of man? How would your relationship with the Word of God change?

PRAYER

That the God of our Lord Jesus Christ, the Father of glory, may give to you the spirit of wisdom and revelation in the knowledge of Him, the eyes of your understanding being enlightened; that you may know what is the hope of His calling, what are the riches of the glory of His inheritance in the saints, and what is the exceeding greatness of His power toward us who believe, according to the working of His mighty power (Eph. 1:17–19)

Father, open the eyes of my understanding, and grant to me the spirit of wisdom and revelation of the knowledge of who You are. Help me to move from living my life solely on sensory knowledge and help me to see and perceive You and Your Word as they truly are. Lord, I repent from thinking Your Word was just a leather book written by men! I now receive it as Your supernatural breath of life, Your will, and the revelation of the essence of who You are. Teach me, lead me, and guide me to live my life through Your holy Word. I ask this in the Name of Jesus Christ! Amen!

ENDNOTE

[1] Oxford English Dictionary (Oxford: Oxford University Press, 1989).

Chapter 3

JESUS, THE WORD OF GOD

THE WORD WAS GOD

In the beginning was the Word, and the Word was with God, and the Word was God. He was in the beginning with God. All things were made through Him, and without Him nothing was made that was made. (John 1:1–3)

Before anything was made for us to see, hear, touch, or taste, the Word of God simply was. It existed "in the beginning," and so it was never created. This means the Word of God existed with God in a realm that pre-existed creation! The Bible could never have been authored by man because it existed before mankind ever was!

Then comes the amazing and life-changing revelation that the Word of God wasn't just with God, didn't just come forth from His mouth, and didn't just exist as a portion of God's knowledge. The Word was actually God! At first, we may have a less than impressive reaction to this revelation because we've probably heard this verse many times. Nevertheless, upon a more serious meditation of it, we may very well begin to see the magnitude of its implications!

It means there's no difference between God and His Word! It means that as God is, so is His Word. As the Word is, so is God. The Word of God is not something that's natural, but is something that's absolutely unequivocally *supernatural!* The Word of God is more than a paperbound book with nice leather and gold-gilded pages. It's more than a collection of "thou shall" and "thou shalt not's." It's more than a theological document for those who study Greek and Hebrew! It's more than anything that can be produced or fully comprehended by mankind! It's the very revelation and manifestation of God Himself, and it's absolutely Heavenly. It's perfect, infallible, indestructible, powerful, and all-knowing! Indeed, the Word *was* and *is* God!

Verse two sheds even more light upon this amazing revelation. It reads:

He was in the beginning with God! (John 1:2)

The Word of God is not presented to us as a "something," but rather is revealed to us as a "someone"! The Word of God is more than the inanimate black leather book we thought it was! The Word of God is referred to as a "He"! It's revealed to us as a Person!

Now we have a clearer picture of the true nature of the Word of God that, thankfully, destroys the common perception of the Bible as being a boring and irrelevant book. People may carry around their Bibles and say they're going to read the Word as if it's a collection of facts, a list of commandments, or a record of historical events. Little do we know that when we're reading the Bible, studying the Bible, and meditating upon God's Word, we're not interacting with a "thing," but rather communing with the very

Person of God Himself! Now of course, the paper, the ink, and the binding of the Bible in book form are all simply natural things. However, the Word of God recorded on its natural pages predates creation, and is actually spiritual in nature and much more than its leather-bound paper. If there was ever a time the expression "Don't judge a book by its cover" applied, it's to the Bible!

> *All things were made through Him, and without Him nothing was made that was made. In Him was life, and the life was the light of men. And the light shines in the darkness, and the darkness did not comprehend it.* (John 1:3–5)

In other words, all things were made through the Word, and without the Word nothing was made. We then see that in "Him," meaning the Word, was life, and the life was the light of men. We learn that the light, which is the Word of God, shines in the darkness, and the darkness didn't comprehend it. The Greek word for "comprehend" is *katalambano,* meaning to overcome, or overtake, or make one's own (Strong's Greek #2638). **In other words, the Bible is revealing that the Word of God is God, that the Word of God creates, that the Word of God is life, and that the Word of God overcomes all evil!** Truly, the Word of God is more than we've understood—its power greater than we've appreciated, and its potential to enable us to live in the supernatural power of God . . . limitless!

THE WORD BECAME FLESH

And the Word became flesh and dwelt among us, and we beheld His glory, the glory as of the only begotten of the Father, full of grace and truth. (John 1:14)

To better get a hold of the reality of the identity of the Word of God, let's consider five revelatory forms of God's Word.

First, because the Word was "in the beginning" and was "with God" and "was God," the Word, therefore, was never created and, therefore, has no author. For something to have an author would mean it had a creator. The "Word was God," and God has no creator, no beginning, and always was.

> *Before the mountains were brought forth, Or ever*
> *You had formed the earth and the world, Even from*
> *everlasting to everlasting, You are God.* (Ps. 90:2)

Certainly, man couldn't have authored it because the Word existed before mankind existed. The Word of God, therefore, is from everlasting to everlasting! Thus, the original form of the Word was nothing at all like anything we can see or perceive. It simply was God, and whatever form God was in was the same form the Word was in. In this form, a human being cannot perceive the Word for it is beyond the realm of our senses. This is what we'll refer to as the "Pre-existent" form of the Word of God. This may be difficult to wrap our heads around, but hold on . . . it's only the beginning!

In Genesis 1:3, we see the second form of the Word of God emerge, which is the "Spoken" Word. This is where the pre-existent Word of God gets released in the form of sound. We'll be talking about the power of the spoken Word in much more detail, but for now, it's enough to consider that the spoken Word is no longer just existing, but moving with clear intention to form, create, and influence. In addition, the spoken Word is a form that can be perceived through our hearing. Thus, God spoke not only to creation, but also to people all through the record of the Bible such as Adam, Eve, Noah, Abraham, kings, prophets, Paul the apostle, and many others. The spoken Word is the revealed Word of God. "Thus says the Lord" occurs approximately 419 times in the Old Testament, "God said" occurs approximately 46 times in the Old Testament and 4 times in the New Testament, and "God spoke" occurs 12 times in the Old Testament and 3 times in the New Testament.[1]

The third form of the Word of God is the "Written" form, which is commonly referred to as "Scripture." This form is probably the most familiar to people as it's what we think about when we think about the Bible. The written form of the Word is the spoken form that has been released in the form of something we can see. Because we have the physical book we call the Bible, which is actually a collection of 66 books, we tend to erroneously view it, discuss it, and study it like most other books. Theologians and scholars alike will often discuss the authorship of each book, the time frame in which it was written, and how we got it, sometimes forgetting its supernatural origin. When we speak of Moses writing the first five books of the Bible; or Matthew, Mark, Luke, and John writing the Gospels; or Peter, Paul, James, and John writing letters, we must never think of them as authors in the traditional sense. We should rather think of them as those who penned God's Word on paper. The Bible boldly declares,

> *knowing this first, that no prophecy of Scripture is of any private interpretation, for prophecy never came by the will of man, but holy men of God spoke as they were moved by the Holy Spirit.* (2 Pet. 1:20–21)

The Bible hasn't been authored by the will or mind of men, but has been revealed to men by the Holy Spirit, who penned the prophecy for all to read and receive! The Bible says in Paul's letter to Timothy:

> *All Scripture is given by inspiration of God, and is profitable for doctrine, for reproof, for correction, for instruction in righteousness, that the man of God may be complete, thoroughly equipped for every good work.* (2 Tim. 3:16–17)

All Scripture, no matter what its form, is "*given* by inspiration of God." In other words, it's revealed to us, not created by us. The word "inspiration" in Greek, *theopneustos,* Strong's Greek #2315, TDNT 6.453,[2] is literally translated, "God-breathed"! This Greek word is a combination of the word "Theos," which means "God," and "Pepneustai," which means "to breathe." It literally means **God-breathed**. All Scripture is the product of God's breath or "God-breathed-ness." God Himself speaks or breathes the Scripture. **All Scripture comes from God's mouth, and emanates from His breath! This is Unleashing Heaven's Breath! It is the very source of His life that gets released through His Word!**

Thus, we *perceive* the pre-existent Word through faith, we *receive* the spoken Word with our ears, and we *study* the written Word with our eyes. In every form of the Word of God, we're nonetheless perceiving, receiving, and studying the very revelation of God Himself!

This leads us to the fourth, and often little understood, form of God's Word, the "Incarnate" Word of God. In John 1:1–3, we saw that the Word of God is not at all an inanimate object. It isn't a "something," but rather a "someone." **This begs the question, "Who is the "He" referred to in these verses? The answer is simple. "He" is Jesus Christ, and He's the perfect revelation of**

God Himself! Jesus was in the beginning, Jesus was with God, and Jesus was God! Jesus was in the beginning with God, and all things were made through Jesus, and without Jesus nothing was made that was made! Jesus is the perfect manifestation of the pre-existent Word, the perfect revelation of the spoken Word, and the perfect fulfillment of the written Word revealed through the Law of Moses and the Prophets!

> *Then He said to them, "These are the words which I spoke to you while I was still with you, that all things must be fulfilled which were written in the Law of Moses and the Prophets and the Psalms concerning Me." And He opened their understanding, that they might comprehend the Scriptures.* (Luke 24:44–45)

The culmination of all three forms of the Word of God came in the living, breathing, incarnate, bodily form of the only begotten Son of God, Jesus Christ! The Bible says about Jesus,

> *And the Word became flesh and dwelt among us, and we beheld His glory, the glory as of the only begotten of the Father, full of grace and truth. John bore witness of Him and cried out, saying, "This was He of whom I said, 'He who comes after me is preferred before me, for He was before me.'" And of His fullness we have all received, and grace for grace. For the law was given through Moses, but grace and truth came through Jesus Christ. No one has seen God at any time. The only begotten Son, who is in the bosom of the Father, He has declared Him.* (John 1:14–18)

Jesus Christ is the Word that became flesh! The Word is now in a form that all can perceive by faith, all can hear speak, and see perform and fulfill all that has been written concerning Him! Jesus Christ is "Unleashing Heaven's Breath." He is that which was God-breathed, and all who heard and saw Him beheld the glory of the Father full of grace and truth! He is the seen fulfillment of all that had been prophesied concerning Him! Jesus is the testimony of the spirit of prophecy! (See Revelation 19:10.)

To behold Jesus Christ is to behold the Word of God, and to behold the Word of God is to behold Jesus Christ! There's no difference! You can't separate God and His Word! To behold the Word of God is to behold the glory as of the only begotten of the Father, and to behold the glory of God is to behold the Word of God! There's no difference! God, His Son, and the Word are one and the same! The Word that was in the beginning and was with God and was God had become flesh when Jesus Christ was born upon the earth in Bethlehem! When we say Jesus Christ was "born" upon the earth, it specifically refers to baby Jesus being born of the virgin Mary. However, Jesus being "born" doesn't mean that Jesus was created, but rather that He was manifested or revealed.

Paul wrote to the Colossians when speaking about Jesus:

> *He is the image of the invisible God, the firstborn over all creation. For by Him all things were created that are in heaven and that are on earth, visible and invisible, whether thrones or dominions or principalities or powers. All things were created through Him and for Him. And He is before all things, and in Him all things consist. And He is the head of the body, the church, who is the beginning, the firstborn from the dead, that in all things He may have the preeminence.* (Col. 1:15–18)

Jesus is the image of the invisible God! He is the visible incarnation of the pre-existent, eternal, God, and all things have been made by and through Him! The writer of the Letter to the Hebrews says,

> *who being the brightness of His glory and the express image of His person, and upholding all things by the word of His power, when He had by Himself purged our sins, sat down at the right hand of the Majesty on high,* (Heb. 1:3)

Jesus' identity is also revealed as the Word of God in the Book of Revelation:

> *His eyes were like a flame of fire, and on His head were many crowns. He had a name written that no one knew except Himself. He was clothed with a robe dipped in blood, and His name is called The Word of God.* (Rev. 19:12–13)

The fifth and final form of the Word of God we'll consider is the "Manifested" form of the Word of God. This is similar to the "incarnate" Word of God, but still yet significantly different. This is where the Word of God becomes "flesh," not in the bodily form of Jesus but in the fulfillment of what it promises. It's the visible manifestation or fruit of what the Word creates. For example, when Jesus cursed the fig tree in Mark 11:13–14;20–21, saying that no one would eat fruit from it again, He released His spoken Word. At first, nothing seemed to happen to the tree. It looked just as healthy as it did. However, the next morning, Peter saw the fig tree, and it was dried up from its roots, and he remembered what Jesus said. The spoken Word became manifested, because it's effect was clearly seen.

An important point concerning the "manifested" form of the Word is that it's released not just by God Himself, but also through human beings! We see God's Word released through men and women in the Old Testament and through the community believers we call the Church in the New Testament. When Jesus released the Great Commission in chapter 16 of the Gospel of Mark, He said,

> *And these signs will follow those who believe: In My name they will cast out demons; they will speak with new tongues; they will take up serpents; and if they drink anything deadly, it will by no means hurt them; they will lay hands on the sick, and they will recover." So then, after the Lord had spoken to them, He was received up into heaven, and sat down at the right hand of God. And they went out and preached every-where, the Lord working with them and confirming the word through the accompanying signs. Amen.* (Mark 16:15–20)

God said that the Word of God would not just be taught by believers, but that signs and wonders would follow those who believe. In other words, the Word of God would be "manifested" through those who believe. They will demonstrate the power of Jesus' Name and the victory of the cross over evil when they cast out demons; they will manifest the promise of the Holy Spirit's coming when they speak in new tongues; they will demonstrate God's divine protection when encountered with danger when they remain unharmed from poison; and they will demonstrate God's power and covenant to heal when they lay hands on the sick and they are healed! The Bible says that the disciples went out and preached everywhere and that Jesus was working with them confirming the Word of God through the accompanying signs. Jesus went with them and confirmed the Word with the manifestations of His Word. Amazingly, the Word of God confirmed the Word of God by producing or "manifesting" what the Word itself promised!

POWER IS RELEASED

If there is only a revelation of the Pre-existent form, the Spoken form, the Written form, and the Incarnate form of the Word of God, but there is no manifestation of that Word, the Word of God has not been fully released! It's as sad and dramatic as a stillborn birth. A beautiful baby full of life was conceived within a womb, and it never came forth to full maturity. It never realized its full destiny.

The apostle Paul said,

> *And my speech and my preaching were not with persuasive words of human wisdom, but in demonstration of the Spirit and of power, that your faith should not be in the wisdom of men but in the power of God.* (1 Cor. 2:4–5)

Paul basically said that he didn't just proclaim things "about" the Word of God with a human level of proficiency to persuade people. He said that his proclamation came with a demonstration or manifestation of the Spirit and power! This was the key that the Corinthians' faith would not be in the wisdom of men, but in the power of God! The Word of God is the power of God, and the power of God, when it's released, is the manifestation of the Word of God!

This form of the Word of God is something we'll spend a great deal of time on because it's at the heart of the Christians' being true witnesses of God upon the earth. The manifested Word of God is vital because it enables the world to experience it's miracle-working power. Again, because the Word of God is God, when the Word of God is manifested, God Himself is manifested! Paul the apostle wrote the believers at Corinth and told them they were living epistles, or letters, that all the world would read and know (see 2 Cor. 3:2–2). They were the manifestation of the God's Word.

God greatly desires for you, your church family, your husband, your wife, your children, your coworkers, and, yes, even your enemies to experience the manifestation of God's Word! God wants *you* to experience the supernatural power of His Word. Remember always that God did more than simply pre-exist! He did more than simply speak. He did more than simply have things written, He sent the incarnation of His Son, Jesus, and manifested the glory of the Word of God by what He did!

When speaking to the Jews who doubted Him, Jesus said,

> *Jesus answered them, "I told you, and you do not believe. The works that I do in My Father's name, they bear witness of Me.* (John 10:25)

SHE TOUCHED THE WORD OF GOD

Now that we have a clear picture that Jesus Christ is the Word of God, let's return one more time to the woman who was healed from the flow of blood. As we shared in Chapter 1, when the woman heard of the report of Jesus, she heard an accurate truth concerning who He was and what He did. She knew He was from God and that He could heal her. She knew in her heart that as soon as she touched Jesus, she would be healed. The result? She was immediately healed!

She accessed Jesus' power through faith. In fact, we saw that even though many people physically touched Jesus, only her supernatural touch caused power to flow. **The simple yet profound reason she was healed was that when she touched Jesus, her faith touched the Word of God!** Her faith made contact with God's promised Word that through Jesus would come healing to all who believed. She received exactly what God provided in His Word!

The Word of God teaches that Jesus Christ was to redeem us from the curse of the law (see Gal. 3:13) and that by His stripes (wounds on His back) we would be physically healed (see Isa. 53:4–5). Although Jesus had not suffered, died, and been raised from the dead, this woman accessed the promise that had already been given by grace through faith in Him!

This is why she didn't need to ask Jesus to make a decision to heal her. The Word of God already settled the issue that healing would be provided to her through Jesus Christ. God had already promised healing to her (and us) in, and through, His Son!

The supernatural transaction that took place occurred between the woman's revelatory faith and the supernatural Word of God! Today, many people touch the physical book we call the Bible and receive very little from it. Those who come to the Word of God receiving, believing, and acting upon the revelation that it's the very revelation of God and His desire will undoubtedly encounter its supernatural power! Let's look at one more example, this time with a desperate mom and her daughter to see this principle in action.

A woman of Canaan came crying to Jesus, begging Him to help her daughter because she was severely demon-possessed. Amazingly, Jesus didn't answer her, and Jesus' disciples urged Him to send her away. What a reception! Here a Gentile woman comes desperately asking Jesus for help and seems to get nothing but rejection (see Matt. 15:23)! Jesus finally answered the woman and told her *". . . I was not sent except to the lost sheep of the house of Israel."* (Matt. 15:24). Even though that it seemed Jesus said no to her request, the woman worshipped Him and continued pleading for His help. Jesus then told her, *". . . It is not good to take the children's bread and throw it to the little dogs."* (Matt. 15:26). The woman responded with complete agreement, and then said something amazing! She said, *"Yes Lord, yet even the little dogs eat the crumbs which fall from their master's table."* (Matt. 15:27). Jesus responds by proclaiming that this Gentile woman had great faith, and permitted her request to be granted!

At first glance, it may appear that Jesus was being overly harsh, and that He said no to the woman; however, a closer look reveals quite the opposite. When this mom came to Jesus, it was the picture of a Gentile coming to the Savior of the Jews. The Bible clearly teaches that Jesus was first sent to the nation of the Jews and then to the Gentiles (see Rom. 1:16). Jesus never said no to the woman, but rather revealed that He was first called to reach the Jews, and then the Gentiles. Thus, Jesus essentially said the blessing that would come to the Gentiles should follow the blessing meant for the Jews. He refers to the Gentiles as "little dogs," but, interestingly, uses the term for a puppy, in contrast to the term for a scavenging dog. The woman agreed with God, but responded to Jesus' comment in a fascinating way when she said that even the little dogs eat the crumbs that fall from their master's table! She declared her faith that the Gentiles would be blessed through the Jews! God's Word when speaking to Abraham, the father of God's chosen people, said,

*I will bless those who bless you, And I will curse him
who curses you; And in you all the families of the earth
shall be blessed."* (Gen. 12:3)

It was at this point that Jesus declared that she had great faith
in the promises that were in Him! She recognized Jesus as the
Messiah because she called Him according to His Messianic title,
the Son of David (see Matt. 15:22)! This woman believed and
received the answer to her blessing because she knew what was
in God's Word. Her faith made contact with the manifested Word
of God and was determined to receive that which was already
promised in Him! She accessed that which was covenanted in
Jesus Christ! She accessed the Word of God!

THE WORD IS OUR SOURCE

*For all the promises of God in Him are Yes, and in Him
Amen, to the glory of God through us.* (2 Cor. 1:20)

As Christians relate to the Word of God properly, supernatural
experiences will begin to emerge just like the woman with the
flow of blood and the Canaanite woman whose daughter became
freed from demonic possession! Many will come to understand
that not only is Jesus Christ the portal into the supernatural realm
of miracles, but that His Word also is just as powerful a portal
because Jesus and His Word are one! They will invest themselves
with a new level of passion and understand that every good and
perfect gift from Heaven can be accessed through God's Word.

There are some Christians who have unfortunately succumbed
to the temptation of the devil to somehow seek the covenanted
blessings of God through methods not found in the Word of God.
They do this by mixing the principles of God's Word with other

things such as new age views and humanistic beliefs such as the power of positive thinking, and some even mix cultic practices with God's Word through the creation of idols, statues, prayer chants, and many more. Even within strong Christian circles of faith, "strange fire" sometimes emerges, releasing darkness into a person's life, attempting to pollute the purity of God's Church. Strange fire, which is spoken of in Leviticus 10:1 (KJV), is essentially unauthorized power that goes before the Lord. It's something that greatly displeases God, and can be extremely dangerous in a person's life. A Christian should have absolutely nothing to do with any "spiritual" thing outside the revelation of God's Word. To drift away from the purity of God's Word is synonymous with drifting away from God! Every Christian who exclusively focuses and clings to God's Word will enjoy the depths of the supernatural realm while allowing no darkness near your dwelling!

Flee from every strange spiritual thing, and understand that nothing needs to be added to the revelation of God's Word. The Gospel of Jesus Christ is more than enough, and all the promises of God are "Yes" and "Amen" in Jesus (see 2 Cor. 1:20). This means the Word of God not only contains every promise meant for your life, but also says "yes" to them! You are blessed by the Father of our Lord Jesus, who has already blessed you with every spiritual blessing in Jesus Christ!

> *Blessed be the God and Father of our Lord Jesus Christ, who has blessed us with every spiritual blessing in the heavenly places in Christ,* (Eph. 1:3)

You are already blessed with the blessing provided to you by Jesus, the Word of God! You can access every promise destined and covenanted to you by Christ and through Christ. In other words, you're meant to receive and enjoy every promise released to you by the Word of God.

You may not be able to touch the physical hem of Jesus' garment, but you're well able to touch the Word of God anytime every day! You have the same access as the woman with the flow of blood because you have been covenanted the same promises!

Hold your Bible in your hand, and consider that you hold the very revelation of God Himself! You hold the portal into the supernatural realm of the Christian life along with all its covenanted blessings, and it's a door that no man can shut! (See Revelation 3:8.)

All can come to God's Word to touch it and apply it! All can hear the Word, read the Word, believe the Word, speak the Word, pray the Word, and encounter its full *power!* Right now, Jesus Christ longs for you to touch Him in the way that will cause power to be released from Him to you!

GOD CONFIRMS HIS WORD

And they went out and preached everywhere, the Lord working with them and confirming the word through the accompanying signs. Amen. (Mark 16:20)

While ministering the true identity of the Word of God in a large meeting in the Dominican Republic, the service was coming to a close, and I sensed God wanted everyone to receive the invitation to touch Him just like the woman with the flow of blood. There wasn't time or room enough to pray for everyone with the laying on of hands, so I directed people to begin praying and receiving God's promise of healing with the same supernatural faith-touch. The woman had the hem of Jesus garment as her touch point, and we had the Name of Jesus as ours.

I distinctly remembered feeling great resistance from the enemy as he attempted to barrage my mind with thoughts of fear and doubt. "What if nothing happens?" "What if people don't believe?". . . "What If I don't believe?" "What if God's Word doesn't work?" These "what if's" are desperate attempts of the enemy to try to prevent us from pressing through the crowds on our way to touch Jesus. We often have to "press" through before we can "break" through, and I knew that as a minister I had to press through so others could break through!

The crowd began to pray with great fervency as they approached Jesus in the Spirit. Finally, I declared with a great shout to receive God's Word of promise of healing in the Name of Jesus Christ! I immediately invited all those who were touched in their bodies to come forward. What happened next really tested my faith because no one seemed to move for what seemed like an eternity, though it was probably only ten seconds. As a new level of doubt attempted to rise within me, it was squashed by the conviction of the power of spiritually believing, receiving, and acting upon the Word of God! I once again invited for all those who were healed to come forward to testify to the glory of God, and said that what had happened to the woman with the flow of blood more than 2,000 years ago also happened today. All of a sudden, a woman in the top back row jumped up and shouted, "My legs are healed!" as she began jumping and dancing around trying out her new legs. Then 5 more, 10 more, 20 more, and so on came forward to testify they had touched God's Word and were healed! They had participated in that spiritual faith-transaction that enabled them to receive the blessings found in Jesus Christ!

Following the service, I was escorted to a large room for a time of fellowship with my brothers and sisters in Christ. One of the elders of the church, a tall, grey-haired gentleman, came and said, "Pastor Steve, you may not have known it, but there was a woman here tonight who suffered greatly from the same condition as the woman with the flow of blood in the Bible.

The woman came and told me that her flow of blood immediately stopped when the prayer went forth to touch Jesus!" I looked at him in awe of the grace and mercy of God because I knew the Lord demonstrated to all of us that He's the same yesterday, today, and forever (see Heb. 13:8)!

This is what we all desperately need! We need to know that God has never changed and never will change! We need to hear and see the same pure, unadulterated report of Jesus Christ just like the woman with the flow of blood in the Gospel of Matthew! This report is so powerful, so convincing, so undeniable that it overwhelms every fear, failure, and frustration we've ever suffered under. This report is so penetrating that it creates unshakable faith and enables us to touch Jesus and cause power to be released from Him the way this "certain" woman did. We need to receive Jesus with the certainty that she did. We need to act upon the report of Jesus the way she did. The Word of God was not meant to be put under a microscope, but was meant to press through a crowd and touch Him!

We need God to breathe His Word into our being so Heaven may pierce our hearts and breathe His life into us. God desires to do it! If you listen closely to the heartbeat of His will, He can't wait for you to receive His pure Word to you so you may touch Him in ways that release His supernatural power into your life! Right now, as you read this, Jesus Christ longs for you and me to touch Him in a way that causes His power to flood our lives!

Chapter Summary Points

1. The Word of God is not presented to us as a "something," but rather is revealed to us as a "someone"! The Word of God is more than the inanimate black leather book we thought it was! The Word of God is referred to as a "He"! It's revealed to us as a Person! Jesus Christ is revealed to us as the Word of God!

2. There are essentially five basic forms of the Word of God. The first is the "pre-existent" form of the Word of God, the second is the "spoken" form of the Word of God, the third is the "written" form of the Word of God, the fourth is the incarnate form of the Word of God, and the fifth is the "manifested" form of the Word of God. According to John 1:14, the Word became flesh, and when we see Jesus, we see the fulfillment of every Word spoken of Him! To behold Jesus Christ is the same as to behold the Word of God, and to behold the Word of God is to behold Jesus Christ! There's no difference! You can't separate God and His Word!

3. When the woman with the flow of blood touched Jesus, her hand touched the hem of His cloak, but her faith touched the covenanted promise in the Word of God! A spiritual transaction took place between her faith and God's Word.

4. When the Canaanite woman believed and held onto her faith that the Gentiles would be blessed through Abraham she accessed God's promise through her faith.

5. The Word of God contains every blessing and promise meant for the child of God. A Christian should cling to God's Word and remain anchored in it. There should never be any mixture in the walk of faith with anything that is outside God's

will in His Word. This will protect every follower of Christ from strange spiritual experiences and ensure they walk in the supernatural blessings of Christ!

6. God confirms His Word as He is still healing people today just as He did more than 2,000 years ago! Jesus is the same yesterday, today, and always! (See Hebrews 13:8.)

QUESTIONS FOR REFLECTION

1. What changes would result in your faith-life by discovering that the Word of God is revealed not as a "something," but as a "someone." How would your relationship with the Word of God change for the better?

2. Think about the five forms of the Word of God. How is the grace of God revealed in the progression from the "pre-existent" form to the "manifested" form of the Word of God?

3. What promises in the Word does God desire for you to access in Him? What desires of your heart do you long to receive from Jesus? How can your faith access God's Word so you can receive the fullness of God's blessings?

4. Think about your faith and your faith-walk. Have you or your loved one ever mixed the pure teaching of the Word of God with things taught outside the Word of God? If so, how? Begin to pray for your loved one, or begin to personally repent from allowing any strange thing to be mixed with the Word of God. Renounce all things outside God's Word, and commit to walking in the purity of God's Word.

5. What things do you have to press through so you can break through into the promised land of God's blessing? How is

Hebrews 13:8 good news for you today, for your family, for your marriage, and for your destiny?

PRAYER

Father, I receive that Jesus was in the beginning, and that Jesus was with You, and that Jesus is the Word of God. I receive that the Word became flesh and that when we look at the Word of God, we see Your glory, Father! I declare that I'm going to walk with a new spiritual perspective of Your Word. When I see Your Word, I will see Your Son, Jesus, and when I see Your Son Jesus, I will see Your Word! I purpose to live my life by communing with Your Word in faith! Father, I declare that You and Your Word will be my sole source of spiritual blessing, I receive that Jesus Christ is the same yesterday, today, and always, and believe that I receive my miracle here and now today by receiving, believing, and acting upon Your mighty Word! I ask this in the Name of Jesus Christ! Amen!

ENDNOTES

[1] Statistics from the *NASB Bible: 1995 Update.*

[2] Gerhard Kittel, Gerhard Friedrich, and Geoffrey W. Bromiley, *Theological Dictionary of the New Testament,* 10th ed. (Wm. B. Eerdmans Publishing Co, 1984).

Chapter 4

RELEASING SUPERNATURAL POWER WHEN GOD SPEAKS

In the beginning God created the heavens and the earth.
The earth was without form, and void; and darkness
was on the face of the deep. And the Spirit of God was
hovering over the face of the waters. Then God said,
"Let there be light"; and there was light. (Gen. 1:1–3)

The first four verses of the Bible reveal that God created the Heavens and the earth. We learn that the earth was void and darkness was on the face of the deep and the Spirit of God hovered over the face of the waters. The full meaning of this verse contains great mystery, but we know there was a realm, where things were not yet fully ordered according to God's glory. The power of God was present hovering over the face of the waters. We also know that darkness was present in this realm as it was on the face of the deep. People sometimes mistakenly think this "light" and "darkness" referred to natural light and darkness, but this isn't the case. God was actually referring to spiritual light and darkness. God hadn't yet created the natural lights such as the sun, moon, and stars until verses 14–18. These verses reveal the beginning of creation and the reality that both God's power and evil were existent in this time and space.

Then something amazing happened. The Bible records that God "**said.**" The simplicity of it is easily overlooked, but it's monumental to understanding the releasing of God's power. God didn't simply "think" light into existence, or "wave his hand" to bring light into existence. He **spoke** it into existence. God said, "Let there be light," and there was light.

The power of God was released when the might or "potential" power of His "pre-existent" form was converted into the moving or "kinetic" form of His "spoken" Word. When the Bible says that the "Spirit of God" was hovering over the face of the waters, the word "Spirit" in Hebrews is *Ruach* (Strong's Hebrew #7307). When God spoke, He released that which was inside Him! He released His Spirit! The power that was within Him moved from Him into the cosmos!

The very well-known verse in 1 John 1:5 reads:

This is the message which we have heard from Him and declare to you, that God is light and in Him is no darkness at all.

The verse reveals that not only does God contain light, but that He Himself is light, and there's absolutely no darkness within Him at all! **When God said, "Let there be light," He literally infused Himself into the cosmos!** In other words, God saw the earth was without form and void and spiritual darkness was on the face of the deep and God desired to release His presence in an intentional way so that He and His glory would become infused into the realm during creation! When God speaks His Word, He releases His very essence! Truly God and His Word are one! For God to release His Word is for Him to release His glory! For Him to release His glory is for Him to release His Word. There is no difference! (See John 1:14.)

POTENTIAL AND KINETIC POWER

I believe there are three pretty rough things in life. The first is forgetting a password to access important information, the second is forgetting your ATM code while standing in front of the machine, and the third is locking your keys inside your car in the middle of nowhere while it's running! These are comical examples, but we become frustrated because we can't access what's ours. We know we're so close, yet so far away from getting what we need.

The reality is that many Christians live their lives like this every day. They go to church; they hear about the promises of God, but they have difficulty accessing them. They're so close, yet so far away from the things they need! The truth is that no matter what door you need opened, you need the right key! Even the largest iron-clad prison doors, though they weigh hundreds of pounds, are opened with keys that weigh less than an ounce! Having the right key changes everything, and unlocking God's miracle power is just the same! Understanding and applying the right spiritual keys in your life will gain you access to things you've only dreamed of! It causes the answers to prayers you've prayed for years to be released in moments! When the storms of life come, we need to be equipped with the spiritual keys that release power in the midst of our need. To do this, we need to understand how to release the supernatural power of God's Word.

Although we've covered that God's power is literally every-where, it doesn't mean that His power is always manifested. In science, there's a big difference between potential and kinetic energy. With potential energy, an object has the "potential" to be able to accomplish something, but the power is dormant. It's present, but not moving. With kinetic energy, the power is not just present, but also moving. An easy illustration of this is a bullet leaving the chamber of a gun. When a bullet is inside a working gun, there's potential energy. However, until the trigger is pulled to cause the explosion that propels the bullet, it will remain harmless in the gun. Once the trigger is pulled, the power is released, and the bullet races out of the gun at an amazing speed. In very much the same way, the potential of God's power is everywhere, but its "kinetic" energy isn't released until the "trigger" is pulled.

LIGHT OVERCOMES DARKNESS

And God saw the light, that it was good; and God divided the light from the darkness. (Gen. 1:4)

When God said, "Let there be light," He intentionally released Himself into the place where spiritual darkness existed. God released God into the cosmos, and it pierced everything! God's Word moved creation! There was no debate, no analysis, no question, and no contending power. Everything simply reacted to the sovereignty of God's authoritative Word.

When God saw the light, He saw that it was good because He saw His Word! He saw Himself! He saw His own image. Because God is light and in Him there is no darkness (see 1 John 1:5), the light (God) and the dark (evil) could not coexist and so they became divided! When God released Himself, every dark thing was overcome! What a powerful picture that God's Word moves from simply being "present" to being "released" causing darkness to retreat!

This is exactly why the movement of God's Word is so vital in our lives. It's more important than just gaining knowledge or doing complex analysis of the Greek and Hebrew languages. It's more than simply influencing our emotions into a peaceful place with morning devotionals. When the Word of God is released, God Himself is released! His authoritative Word separates light from dark and good from evil. It destroys the void and causes all things to be ordered according to His glory!

We see this same parallel in the Gospel of John when we are introduced to the Word of God and its effect on creation. The Bible says,

> *All things were made through Him, and without Him nothing was made that was made. In Him was life, and the life was the light of men. And the light shines in the darkness, and the darkness did not comprehend it.* (John 1:3–5)

All things were made by the Word and the Word was the life, or light of men, and the light shines in the darkness and the darkness did not overcome it! Both "in the beginnings" in Genesis and the Gospel of John demonstrate a release of God's Word with the same effect! Light destroys darkness!

Sickness, disease, depression, anxiety, and every other form of darkness flee when God's light is released! How does God release His light? The same way He did in Genesis . . . He releases His Word!

DEMONS FLEE IN AFRICA

I was recently ministering in a wonderful church in Ghana, Africa, near the capital city of Accra. The congregation was filled with joy during their time of worship. Men, women, and children jumped, danced, and shouted praises to God. As I worshipped the Lord with them, I felt Jesus desired for me to share these wonderful truths concerning the light of God's Word. As I began to minister, I saw heads begin to nod in agreement as I saw the revelation of the power of God's spoken Word begin to be understood. I knew the Holy Spirit was making His truth clear to His people. At the end of the message, I gave an altar call for people to receive the grace and love of Jesus along with an invitation to release God's Word so He could separate the light from the dark in their lives. It seemed the entire church came to the altar ready to speak forth God's Word during our time of prayer! They were hungry to receive all that God desired for them to have.

During our prayer time, I began to lay hands on them and simply spoke God's Word over them, and as always, God's Word accomplished what He sent it to do. People who had pain in their bodies testified that there was no longer any pain. A woman with a back condition was healed. A woman with pain in her head was healed. Another woman with pain in her knee was healed. One after another, the Word of God, which is the perfect image of God, was released through the spoken Word. One woman who seemed as quiet as could be came forward for prayer and said nothing. As prayer went forth in Jesus' Name, her body began to shake violently as an unclean spirit began to manifest. In only a few moments, that evil spirit left her body, and she was at peace in the presence of Almighty God. Light always overcomes darkness!

God gracefully demonstrates this principle every day to the entire world. Every night following a time of darkness the sun rises, releases light, and destroys the darkness. Even when one hemisphere experiences the dead of the night, the sun is still shining in another. No one ever questions whether the sun has been destroyed or whether the sun lacks power to overcome darkness. We simply understand that as the earth becomes positioned properly, it will be exposed to the light and the darkness will flee. In just the same way, we sometimes experience the reality that evil is present. Although we go through difficult times, we must remember that the light of the Son of God, His Word, is always shining. Anything that's been touched by the enemy's power of darkness needs to be exposed to the released power of God's Word. We simply need Jesus, whose name is the Morning Star, (see Revelation 2:28; 22:16) to arise and divide the light from the dark!

All too often people speak about the Bible, study the Bible, and even celebrate the great revelations of the Bible never encountering more than its "potential" power. In contrast, others will activate the miracle-working power of God's Word by speaking it with faith, releasing its "kinetic" power and causing darkness to scatter.

Have no fear. When God speaks, He releases Himself and overcomes evil. If you're in darkness, or if your body is sick, it's time your problem was exposed to the light of God's Word. It never fails and it always overcomes darkness!

GOD SENT HIS WORD

Then Jesus spoke to them again, saying, "I am the light of the world. He who follows Me shall not walk in darkness, but have the light of life." (John 8:12)

To get an even clearer picture of these truths, it will be helpful to see the releasing of God's Word in the context of God's big story, also known as the metanarrative of Scripture. Doing this will help us see that the events that took place in Genesis 1:1–4 were a prophetic picture of what was to take place in the Gospel of Jesus Christ!

In Genesis, we learn that the earth was void and darkness was on the face of the deep. After the Fall of Man into sin, the earth became cursed and all who were in it. It became void of God and filled with darkness (evil). In Genesis, we see that God said, "Let there be light," and the light was sent forth into the darkness ultimately separating light from the dark. We saw that God sent His Word to overcome the darkness! In the Gospel of John, we read that

> *In the beginning was the Word, and the Word was with God, and the Word was God.[2] He was in the beginning with God.[3] All things were made through him, and without him was not any thing made that was made.[4] In him was life, and the life was the light of men.[5] The light shines in the darkness, and the darkness has not overcome it.* (John 1:1–5, ESV)

We can now see the parallel that Jesus, who is God's Word, is revealed as the light of God, who overcomes darkness! The beauty of this picture unfolds as we look at one of the most well-known verses in the Bible:

> *For God so loved the world that He gave His only begotten Son, that whoever believes in Him should not perish but have everlasting life.* (John 3:16)

God so loved the world that He gave His only begotten Son! Who is this Son of God? He is the Word of God who was with God in the beginning! He is the revelation of the light! He is the revelation of God Himself! God sent His Son into the world to give us light, separate us from evil and to be joined to Him! The Bible declares that whoever believes in Jesus will not perish but have everlasting life! They will no longer live in darkness, but will live in His light of life! This is further confirmation that the darkness spoken of here is not natural darkness but is spiritual darkness. Jesus wasn't saying that we would walk in natural light if we followed Him, but in spiritual light! In other words, we would be walking in God Himself! Truly, God is light and in Him there is no darkness!

Let us grab this revelation and receive it deeply into our being. There is no mixture between light and dark. God sent His Word to us to deliver us from every form of darkness. When we follow Jesus, which is the same as following His Word, then we will live with an uncommon level of purity and power! We will live in light, and we will not live in darkness! Great change comes to all who receive Jesus Christ and live according to Him and His Word!

Jesus even told the devil, *". . . It is written, 'Man shall not live by bread alone, but by every word that proceeds from the mouth of God.'"* (Matt. 4:4, see also Deut. 8:3). He was declaring that man should live according to the Word of God and not according to anything else! This is the key that opens the biggest of doors and moves the tallest of mountains! If there is no mixture of light and dark in God, then there's no mixture of light and dark in His Word, and then there will be no mixture in your life when you live according to it! You will not walk in darkness, but will have the light of life (John 1:5)!

GOD'S WORD SENT TO ALL

He sent His word and healed them, And delivered them from their destructions. (Ps. 107:20)

The foundation of the Christian life must be that which God sent to us if we are to stand in strength and success. Our foundation must be sure, solid, and steadfast in God. When we receive that which God sent to us and follow it, we'll find our feet firmly established upon the rock, which is Christ!

God sent His Word in the form of light in Genesis, and He sent His Word in the form of Jesus (see John 1:14) in the Gospel of John. Our job is to receive what He sent, believe it, and act upon it. Our job is to fully embrace the complete revelation of the Word of God in its supernatural form so we may benefit from all that it contains!

The Good News is that God doesn't have a giving problem! From the very beginning, God has proven Himself to be the greatest giver in all creation even in the worst of times! When Adam and Eve sinned, they made insufficient coverings, and so God sacrificed an animal to make clothes from the skins so they could properly be covered. When God sent a flood to the earth to destroy sinful man, Noah found grace in the eyes of God, and God gave Noah perfect building plans to construct the ark. When the nation of Israel was released from bondage in Egypt, God gave His chosen people all their gold. When Israel had no idea how to live with God and how to abide with Him, God gave Moses the Ten Commandments. When God desired His presence to dwell among the people, God gave Moses the plans for the Ark of the Covenant. When Israel needed to be delivered from enemies, God raised up judges with military skill and might to deliver them. When the human race needed to be delivered from their sin, God gave His only begotten Son, Jesus Christ, to suffer, die, be buried, and rise on the third day so we could become the sons and daughters of God. When people needed to be healed of sickness and disease, God gave Jesus' back to be whipped and beaten (see Isa. 53:4–5).

The amazing thing about God's generosity concerning the giving of His Son, Jesus, is that no one ever convinced God to do it! Think of it . . . no one actually asked God to sacrifice His Son upon the cross. It was God's idea! Even more, the Bible tells us that it was God's good pleasure to bruise His Son!

> *Yet it pleased the Lord to bruise Him; He has put Him to grief. When You make His soul an offering for sin, He shall see His seed, He shall prolong His days, And the pleasure of the Lord shall prosper in His hand.* (Isa. 53:10)

The Bible says,

> *What then shall we say to these things? If God is for us, who can be against us? He who did not spare His own Son, but delivered Him up for us all, how shall He not with Him also freely give us all things?* (Rom. 8:31–32)

If God didn't spare His own Son for us, but delivered Him to be sacrificed for us, how shall He not freely give us all things? Reject every fearful lie that God doesn't desire to bless you! God sent His Word to heal you and to deliver you! He sent His Word so that all could access Him; all could know Him; and all could be saved, healed, and delivered! God crushed His Son, Jesus, so that all could be made whole in every way! He desires to get His return on His Son's blood, and because He died for all, He desires all to be made whole!

God is excited for our perception of His Word to change. He's excited that we would no longer look at His Word as a mere leather-bound book. He's excited that we would see that He and His Word are one and that He sent Himself in the form of His Word, who became flesh to crush the devil and restore us back to Him!

How could we have missed so great a truth that God desires to give before we even ask? How could we still be wondering whether it's God's will to provide, God's will to heal, or God's will to save? The answer is that for many generations we've allowed the reason of religious traditions authored by men to pastor us rather than the supernatural love of God revealed in His Word.

God longs for us to know Him more intimately than anyone else. He desires for us to abide in Him and His Word so that we'll live as one with Him. Like Thomas, Jesus would tell us to place our hands into His wounds so that we may believe (see John 20:27). In the same way, God is calling for us to go deeper into His Word so that we may touch the revelation of Jesus and come to a new and unshakable level of faith.

REST ASSURED

"For all those things My hand has made, And all those things exist," Says the Lord. "But on this one will I look: On him who is poor and of a contrite spirit, And who trembles at My word." (Isa. 66:2)

If you've ever been intimidated or afraid you may not be smart enough to understand the Bible, rest assured that you're well able to understand and grasp every Word that proceeds from the mouth of God. The Bible is not understood through human intellect, but is revealed through God-given, heart-received revelation. If you think you haven't been a believer long enough to understand the Bible, don't fret; God's grace enables both the new and the experienced to receive His revelation! If you think you're not the "student type" don't worry. The Bible wasn't given for academic study; it was given for life-transformation. A person may have an IQ that's off the charts, been around Christianity for nine decades, and studied theology all their life, and have nothing more than a lot of impressive information. However, the person who has a humble and contrite spirit and receives the Bible as the very Word of God and respects it to such a degree that they "tremble" before it will receive the keys to spiritual treasures never experienced by the masses.

It's time to do more than just read the Bible. It's time to hear the heart and voice of God emanating from His Heavenly throne. It's time to receive God's supernatural revelation and to abide, or dwell, in His Word. It's time to be so reliant upon God's Word that it's like the air we breathe. It's time for us to breathe Unleashing Heaven's Breath.

Take a deep breath, and allow your mind to soak in the following verse. Take time for it to sink in, and let it nourish you. Like a soft summer rain falling into rich soil, let the truth that God's Word will free you fill and consume every part of your being! The Father has already accepted you, and His love will hold nothing back from you! His Word releases His supernatural power into your life and sets you free!

> *Then Jesus said to those Jews who believed Him, "If you abide in My word, you are My disciples indeed. And you shall know the truth, and the truth shall make you free." (John 8:31–32)*

CHAPTER SUMMARY POINTS

1. God's power is everywhere but there exists His "potential", or might and His "kinetic", or moving power. The Word of God may be everywhere, but its supernatural power needs to be released.

2. God released the power of His Word through the act of speaking it. When He speaks, He releases Himself because He is the Word of God.

3. When God releases His Word, His presence is released and it separates light from darkness. The darkness in our lives will flee as the power of the Word of God is released in and through us.

4. God sent His Word and healed His people! All who receive the Word of God can receive the benefits contained in it!

5. The sending of God's Word in the New Testament is synonymous with the sending of Jesus Christ to the earth! Jesus is God's Word, and Jesus is the light of the world sent to deliver me from spiritual death and darkness.

6. God's Word is sent to all so all can be saved, healed, and delivered!

7. God's Word is not understood through intellectual ability, but by coming to God with a humble, contrite, and teachable heart.

QUESTIONS FOR REFLECTION

1. Have I allowed the Word of God to get planted within me? Has it been lying dormant within me? Am I willing to release

the supernatural power of God's Word through prayer, confessions, and other forms of speaking God's Word?

2. What does God's Word say about the darkness in my life? Will I allow God's Word to shine into the toughest areas of my life so that He can consecrate all I am for His glory?

3. Do I fully believe that God sent His Word to me so I can glorify Him? Is there part of me that believes the supernatural blessings of God are for someone else? Will I make the decision to trust God and take Him at His Word that He loves me and is willing to bless me through His Word?

4. Have I come to God's Word with a contrite spirit and with an attitude that "trembles" at His Word (see Isa. 66:2)? What attitudes about God's Word do I need to reinforce and what attitudes about God's Word do I need to repent of?

PRAYER

Father, I thank You and praise You that you spoke Yourself into creation for me! I thank You that You sent Jesus Christ, the Light of the world, to rescue and save me! Lord let Your light shine in me and through me! Help me to receive, believe, and act upon Your Word so Your light can cast away all demonic things that attempt to influence my life. Help me to have a humble and contrite spirit that trembles at Your Word so I may live and walk with a revelatory understanding of Your holy Word and live according to its supernatural power for Your Glory! I ask this in the Name of Jesus Christ! Amen!

Part II

ENCOUNTERING POWER

Chapter 5

GOD HEARS OUR CRY

THE RELIGION I KNEW

Like so many, I grew up attending church hearing snippets of Gospel truth, but for the most part, I encountered religious traditions that, though well-intended, never really led me to encounter the living, breathing, hearing, seeing, and feeling God of creation. Instead, these traditions created an impression of a God who loved me, but who nevertheless was still the God "out there somewhere." It was normal to see people go to church, follow the same exact order of service each week, say the same things, sing the same songs, and see nothing supernatural. It was as if we were following a protocol on earth saturated with ceremonies, symbols, and memorials of Heavenly things, but we could never get too close because it was all somehow untouchable. It was too far away and too unattainable. Heaven and all the beauty spoken of was a distant hope except for those who have already left this life and gone on to be with Jesus. The rest of us were to plod through this life praying and hoping that God would have mercy on us sinners. If you needed help, you could pray, hope that God heard, and "look to the end of your own wrist" for tangible help.

The whole religious process was meant to bring comfort and hope, but it left an impression that suffering was a normal and necessary part of life we had to endure for some greater good. I saw many pray for help, but they had little expectation that anything would change because they figured the pain in their lives was simply part of God's plan they needed to accept. They believed miracles happened a long time ago when Jesus walked the earth, and weren't things anyone should expect to happen today—at least not to them. People tried to follow what they learned, to live a good life and be a good person, and hope that God would somehow have mercy on their best efforts to "make it" through. Then, you hoped you did more good than bad before you died and hoped to "make" it to Heaven. This of course never bothered me because it was all I knew. In fact, it's all anyone in my circle of friends and family ever knew. It was just the way things were. In fact, I was quite content and never deeply longed for anything more. I never expected anything more because it never even entered my head . . . that is . . . until I was diagnosed . . . with *cancer* as a teenager.

THE BAD NEWS

At the age of 19, while vacationing at the beach, I woke up one morning and noticed an egg-sized lump on the right side of my neck. I didn't immediately worry about it because I often experienced swollen glands when sick. The two peculiar things were that the lump was about the size of an egg and I didn't at all feel sick. I went to my friends and family, and no one truly believed it was anything to be concerned about. After waiting one week to see if the lump would diminish in size, we realized it never got smaller. We went to a doctor, who prescribed antibiotics, and were told to see him in two weeks. Two weeks passed, and the lump still didn't get smaller. We went for further testing, and the doctors believed it to be a cyst or an abscess (infection). The doctors explained the only sure way to diagnose the mass was to perform a biopsy. Following three days of agonized waiting, I received the results of the biopsy, and it was positive for cancer. I was so devastated I had difficulty comprehending the meaning of the word "positive" in the test results. It was as if my mind wanted to hear the results were positive as in "good" even though I knew it really meant I had cancer. My reaction to the news was less than anything to brag about. I began screaming, kicking, and punching anything and everything in my sight. Horrible thoughts of pain and death rushed through my mind with uncontrollable speed.

GOD HEARD

In my distress I called upon the Lord, And cried out to my God; He heard my voice from His temple, And my cry came before Him, even to His ears. (Ps. 18:6)

Shortly following the initial shock of learning I had cancer, I began receiving a battery of tests to determine where the cancer had spread and what damage it may have already caused. It was during a brief break from these tests was I able to spend a weekend at a beautiful remote beach to think and sort things out.

It was late in the afternoon, and everyone had left the beach. It was me, the sand, and the God I thought was "somewhere out there." As I sat in the sand, I looked out into the sky and prayed two words that changed my life. I prayed, **"Teach me."** Before this time, I prayed to a God, but wasn't really sure of who He was.

I had previously learned to recite prayers rather than to freely talk with God, but the need to understand what was happening to me and how to overcome it was so strong that it caused me to pray from my heart. I wanted to understand why I had cancer and how to overcome it. I had no idea what impact that simple prayer would have on my life. Not only did God hear me, but He was ready to answer me!

Living in America and growing up around religion, I heard the Name of Jesus many times. In fact, I even considered myself to be a believer in Jesus Christ. Little did I know that when I cried out to God for help that He was going to introduce Himself to me as He really was . . . not as most would have explained Him, but as He really is—a God of love who not only desires to heal, but will heal and does heal. A God who has been seeking us long before we ever thought to seek Him. A God who is faithful and ready to reveal Himself to all who ask, seek, and knock (see Matt. 7:7–11). A supernatural God who is both able and willing to perform signs, wonders, and miracles. A God who isn't a God of yesterday, but a God who is an ever-ready-present help right now (see Ps. 46:1). A God who's intimate, personal, and filled with more love toward us than we've ever known. A God who released His knowledge, will, and power through His Word.

GOD'S ANSWER

About three months later, I met a humble man who lived nearby my home. In the course of our conversation, I told him I had cancer, and he gave me a warm, reassuring smile. He then slid an old, well-worn, black leather book across the desk. I looked, and to my surprise, it was the Holy Bible. Not understanding what he was trying to tell me, I awkwardly said something like, "What does this have to do with me being sick?" I'll never forget his response. He leaned across the desk, looked deeply into my eyes, and softly said, "**Everything.**" He said it with such certainty, with such conviction, and with such assurance; I knew this man had something I desperately needed. As strange as it may sound, I knew he was somehow not a common person. There was a peace, a power, and a presence that was so restful and strong. The way he spoke about the Bible was also something I had never encountered. He seemed to understand there was something special about that book that most didn't at all know about.

We met on a Friday afternoon soon after our first encounter, and he shared a piece of wisdom with me I never forgot. He said, "If you want to find God, don't ask man . . . ask God." His statement made too much sense to ignore and I was ready to listen to God's Word about God, about satan, and about sickness and disease. One Bible verse after another, I learned that God is not only the creator of the universe, but also the creator of my life! I learned I had something called sin and that it caused me to be separated from God, and was at the heart of *all* my troubles. In fact, I walked in knowing that I had cancer and then came to learn I was a sinner headed for hell!

GOD'S PROMISE

Christ has redeemed us from the curse of the law, having become a curse for us (for it is written, "Cursed is everyone who hangs on a tree"), that the blessing of Abraham might come upon the Gentiles in Christ Jesus, that we might receive the promise of the Spirit through faith. (Gal. 3:13–14)

Like most people, I thought I was a "good" person. I had never killed anyone, and I tried to live a good life. The problem was that I determined "goodness" by my own standards rather than by God's standard. His standard of "good" is His law found in the Ten Commandments. I came to understand that because I had told lies, I was a "liar"; because I had stolen, I was a "thief"; because I hadn't always loved God first in my life, I was an "idolater"! By comparing myself with God's level of perfection, I no longer saw myself as "good." By my own confession, I was a lying, idolatrous thief! I learned that God can't just overlook evil and pretend it isn't there. He doesn't allow liars, adulterers, and the unbelieving into Heaven (see Rev. 21:8).

I learned that God's love provides a way to cleanse and forgive us of our sins. God's Son, Jesus Christ, was sent to suffer for our crimes (sin) so we can be set free from sin. I read in the Bible that if I believed in Jesus Christ, the only begotten Son of God, and accepted His sacrificial death for the forgiveness of my sins, that not only would I become a Heaven-bound child of God, but that God's promises through Jesus Christ would heal me of sickness and disease!

I had learned that God was powerful and a God of love, but never realized He would send His power to flow from His throne directly into my heart, mind, and body! Bible verse after Bible verse demonstrated the Father in Heaven not only loved me, but also wanted to bless me in every way imaginable. Yes, God is able to do exceedingly and abundantly more than we could think or even ask (see Eph. 3:20)! I learned that through Jesus Christ, God the Father made a promise that we would be free from the curse of sin, and therefore free from the resulting troubles of sickness, disease, fear, anxiety, and any other type of oppression. Here is what I read from the Bible.

Surely He has borne our griefs And carried our sorrows; Yet we esteemed Him stricken, Smitten by God, and afflicted. But He was wounded for our transgressions, He was bruised for our iniquities; The chastisement for our peace was upon Him, And by His stripes we are healed. (Isa. 53:4–5)

These are more than fancy words! They boldly declare that God sent Jesus Christ to take our griefs and sorrows! That He was sent to rescue us from the consequences of the curse of sin and death. In Hebrew, the word "griefs" is translated, "chŏlîy" (Strong's Hebrew #2483), which means "sickness", and the word "sorrows" is translated "mak'ôb" (Strong's Hebrew #4341), meaning "pain"! God sent Jesus to take our curse which results from sin and give us freedom that results from His righteousness!

GOD'S PROVISION

As I sat and learned these great promises of God, my heart and mind welled up with expectation. I had read parts of the Bible before and even took a couple of theology classes in college. However, I never experienced the clarity of God's Word until that day. This follower of Jesus had me read one verse after another aloud. The power of the words seems to jump off the page and into my heart. I knew they were true; I somehow knew they were not the words of a man. It was as if God was speaking to me.

After about five hours of study, I remember asking this man whether these all meant that I would be healed of cancer. His response was simply, "It depends on your attitude". He went on to explain that God's Word and the promises that it reveals need to be received by *faith*. With faith, the promises in the Word of God would become reality. Said another way, the Word would move from its "written" form to its "manifested" form when I received it!

The question I was faced with that day was, "Do I really trust God to perform what He promised to do through Jesus Christ?" Knowing that God cannot lie and that the Word of God cut to the very core of my being, I believed (see Heb. 4:12). That day, right then and there, I received Jesus Christ as the Lord and Savior of my life. I believed He died to pay the penalty for my sins upon the cross, and that the Father raised Him up from the dead on the third day. I received the forgiveness of my sin and made a declaration that I would repent (turn away) from sin, and *never* turn back.

Immediately following my new-founded commitment to follow Jesus, this man laid his hands upon my head and commanded the sickness to leave my body in the *Name of Jesus Christ*. My body began to be filled with power from all directions. Though I didn't see detail, I knew a circle of entities formed around us as we prayed. I didn't know it then, but I now understand that they were angels. As God's power came and prayer continued in the Name of Jesus Christ, my body began to shake, and I finally heard the man say in prayer, "get out in the Name of Jesus Christ!" All of a sudden I found myself lying on the ground completely at rest and peace. I remember thinking to myself, "This peace is amazing"! After a while, I stood up from the floor and it was as if electricity was running through my body, and it continued for some time! I knew God had healed me in the *Name of Jesus Christ*. I knew I was clean and healthy again!

Following this amazing experience, the doctors ran tests and found no sign of cancer! Even damage caused from radiation was reversed! **I was 100% healed by the prayer of faith in the Name**

of Jesus Christ of Nazareth! Through this experience, I came to understand the power of God's Word—not only to heal me from sickness and disease, but that every Word that proceeds from the mouth of God is worthy to live by (see Matt. 4:4)!

Before that day, if someone asked me whether I believed that Jesus Christ was the Son of God, I would have said "yes." However, I was familiar only with the idea of Jesus through religious traditions I experienced in church. I had no knowledge of God's Word concerning who Jesus Christ really is and what He accomplished on the cross. Before that day, I never had an encounter with the Word of God.

When I sat on that beach and asked God to teach me, I didn't feel much of anything. There were no lightning bolts from the sky, no earthquakes, and no grand visions. In fact, it appeared nothing much happened at all. However, God heard my cry, and He introduced me to the most powerful thing in all creation . . . His Word!

NO PARTIALITY

For there is no partiality with God. (Rom. 2:11)

When people hear of either my testimony of being healed from cancer or the many miracles that have taken place in the lives of others, they sometimes think they are wonderfully encouraging stories, but wish they would finally happen to them! Many people experience feelings of discouragement thinking they're somehow unworthy, their situation is just a little too bad, or that God does not desire to bless them. Sometimes hearing about someone else's blessing even causes pain in the midst of their own unanswered prayer.

God knows our thoughts and fears, and knows how satan attempts to get us to believe that the promises of God are for everyone—except us. The devil will do all that he can to try to prevent us from praying the prayer of faith! But, we must stand strong and see through the lies of satan, and allow the love of God to pierce our very souls, because with God, there is no partiality (see Rom. 2:11)!

We must be determined to break out of what "has been" and focus upon what "will be." Driving a car while staring into a rearview mirror has unpleasant side effects. It's vitally important to see past the past, see past present circumstances, and see into the purity of God's faithful promises. When we see Jesus, and nothing but Jesus, it enables us to be enveloped with His super-natural love. To see Jesus, I mean really *see* Jesus, is to come to understand that His *love* has no partiality. He has no favorites. He loves each person individually, with an everlasting love that's deeper and wider than we know. Amazingly, Jesus said when praying for those who believe,

> *And I have declared to them Your name, and will declare it, that the love with which You loved Me may be in them, and I in them."* (John 17:26)

Jesus desires for the same love the Father loved Jesus to be in us! This is not for a select few but for everyone! The Father shed His Son's blood for everyone, and He desires for everyone to benefit from it! This means that the same love in which He loves me is the same love in which He loves you! When it comes to the promises and covenant God has made with us through Jesus upon the cross at Calvary, what He does for one, He will do for all!

If God desires to bless everyone equally then what's hap-pening? Why are so many Christians struggling to get blessed, and even walk in half the promises of God? The short answer is that though Heaven is giving, earth has difficulty receiving! Whether it be sin, doubt, unbelief, feelings of unworthiness, lack of knowledge, unforgiveness, or other hindrances to God's blessing, the fact is that Heaven still desires for us to walk in the fullness of the blessings that flow from the work of Jesus Christ upon the cross.

If God was unwilling to bless us, there would be nothing that we could do to get blessed. We would have to shrug our shoulders and say well I'll just have to deal with what I'm going through because God must not want me to be well. We'd have to surrender to the situation because God was unwilling to deliver us from it. We wouldn't be able to fight God. However, the fact that God has already decided to bless His children with every spiritual blessing (see Eph. 1:3) means we *never* have to settle for less than God's best. We can decide to change! We can grow, learn, mature, and be cultivated by His Holy Spirit in His Word, and allow Him to transform us and overcome every barrier and hindrance between us and the heritage of our rightful blessings.

We could approach God with a lot of natural striving or we could realize God has already done the work, already bled His blood, and already suffered the things necessary for us to enter in. Refuse to be conformed to this world, and allow God to transform you by the renewing of your mind that you may prove what is that good and acceptable and perfect will of God (see Rom. 12:2). Completely rid your mind of all thoughts and emotions that would attempt to speak the lie that God will bless others but not you. Take time and pray this prayer so you may position yourself to be a receiver of all that God desires for you to have.

Father, I thank you that you show no partiality to people. I thank You that You love me just as much as you love others who walk in your blessings. Help me to know your love more. Help me to understand and receive the fullness of your love for me. Lord, I renounce all agreement with the devil's lies that You don't love me, or won't bless me. Help me never to see my past, but to see You and the great blessings you are leading me into. I receive the fullness of Your love for me. Overwhelm my entire mind, body, and whole being with your love. Make me a testimony and witness of your grace, power, and love to the whole world. I receive it Jesus! Thank you Jesus! Amen.

YOUR ENCOUNTER

To see God produce physical signs and wonders is awesome! He can make the ground shake, the sky shine, and countless other displays of His power. However, the greatest level of encountering God is with His Word. To encounter the Word is to encounter God, and He's the source of every supernatural blessing and display! How wonderful it is to know the source of supernatural power! How wonderful it is to now understand that God's Word is bigger than the leather-bound book we carry around! How wonderful it is to know that God's Word is revealed as the pre-existent Word, the spoken Word, the written Word, the incarnate Word, and the manifested Word!

When the woman with the flow of blood touched Jesus's clothes with faith, she touched the Word of Promise and was immediately healed! You can access God's supernatural power by accessing and believing His Word. If you never believed in Jesus Christ as your Lord and Savior, or never deeply encountered God's Word concerning what it means to be saved, you can do it right now. You can receive God's Word that reveals to us that

> *. . .all have sinned and fall short of the glory of God,* (Rom. 3:23)

You can trust the Word of God when it tells us that

> *For the wages of sin is death, but the gift of God is eternal life in Christ Jesus our Lord.* (Rom. 6:23)

You can trust God when He tells us that

> *. . .if you confess with your mouth the Lord Jesus and believe in your heart that God has raised Him from the dead, you will be saved.* (Rom. 10:9)

It's time to take God at His Word and to choose to believe Him! You can pray this prayer as a guide and receive Jesus Christ, the Word of God, and become filled with His light and life and you will be rescued from all darkness!

Lord Jesus, I know I'm a sinner and have fallen short of Your glory. I know I need forgiveness of my sins, and desire to turn away from my sins. I no longer want to live my life separated from You. I believe You are the only begotten Son of God and that God raised You from the dead on the third day. Please forgive me of my sins in the Name of Jesus Christ! I receive the forgiveness of my sins and accept You as my Savior from sin and death. By faith I receive Your gift of grace and eternal life! Thank you Jesus! I will now follow You all the days of my life as Your disciple (follower)!

If you've prayed this prayer with an honest and believing heart, you've been, without any doubt or question, washed of every sin and wrong you've ever committed. You have been made righteous in God's eyes, and you are ready to receive every spiritual blessings that's in Christ Jesus! Begin looking for a good church that teaches the perfect, infallible Word of God. Go and tell someone of the decision you've made today! Write it down and never forget it! Today is the best day of your life because today you've received eternal life!

CHAPTER SUMMARY POINTS

1. Sometimes we encounter religious things that appear good, but they are not the Word of God. It is important to think about what you believe and where it came from. If it didn't come from the Word of God, it isn't from God.

2. When problems come to us and we cry out to God for help, He is a good, good Father and He hears us when we cry!

3. God's primary method of speaking to us and revealing Himself is to bring us to His Word. His Word reveals who He is and how to receive all that He has prepared for us. His Word is the manner in which He released His blessings to us.

4. For a person to benefit from the Word of God, they must receive God's Word and receive it with faith. They cannot merely have a mental agreement with it. They must receive and believe it in their hearts!

5. The first step that everyone takes is to receive God's Word concerning how to receive Jesus Christ, the Lord of Lords, so that our sins can be washed away, we can be made completely whole and righteous, and we can become his sons or daughters.

QUESTIONS FOR REFLECTION

1. Think about what you've believed for most of your life. What things do you think came from God, and what things do you think came from men? How can you know the difference?

2. Think about the things you've been going through. Have you cried out to God from the bottom of your heart to Him? Why or why not?

3. Most of us are taught that the Bible is important, but have you really received it as God's answer and released to you to overcome? Have you been searching in all the wrong directions or have you been diligently seeking your answers in God's Word?

4. Have you spiritually and powerfully encountered Jesus Christ and His Word in a way that has brought the deepest of transformations to your life? Do you have a relationship with Jesus in a way that you know that He has forgiven you and saved you from your sin?

5. If you haven't already, are you ready to receive God's Son, Jesus Christ, which is the gift of grace that He was willing to die for you on the cross to take away every ounce of punishment for the sins that you've committed? Are you ready to believe and receive God's Word so you can escape hell and receive eternal life? Are you ready to leave your old life of sin and be joined with Jesus Christ?

PRAYER

In my distress I called upon the Lord, And cried out to my God; He heard my voice from His temple, And my cry came before Him, even to His ears. (Ps. 18:6)

Father, You know everything about me. You know my rising up and my lying down. You are Lord and You know every good and bad thing I've been through and are going through. Lord, I'm willing to receive Your Word. I receive it as I receive You! I receive that it is more than a leather-bound book, and I receive that it's the supernatural revelation of who You are. I receive that I should live by every Word that proceeds from Your mouth (see Matt. 4:4). *Lord, please lead and guide me to understand and release Your Word so I may stand in the fullness of Your blessings! In the Name of Jesus Christ I receive it! Amen!*

AUDIO TESTIMONY: STEVE HANNETT

To receive a link to the free audio message of Pastor Steve sharing his testimony of being healed of cancer, please send an e-mail to contact@iwantgrace.org

Chapter 6

THE KINGDOM OF GOD

THE GOSPEL AND THE KINGDOM OF GOD

In this manner, therefore, pray: Our Father in heaven, Hallowed be Your name. Your kingdom come. Your will be done On earth as it is in heaven. (Matt. 6:9–10)

When God sent His Son to the earth, He sent more than a messenger, more than an ambassador, more than just a prophet, more than a teacher, and more than a priest. God sent the King of Heaven Himself! Jesus Christ was sent from Heaven to the earth, and, according to Hebrews 3:1, was the first apostle. At a basic level, it means that Jesus was sent by God, that He had a specific mission, and that He had the power to complete the task. Jesus came through a virgin birth and thus had no spiritual predecessor. He came perfectly representing His Father's will, and did only what He saw His Father do (see John 5:19), and spoke only what He heard His Father speak. Jesus' Kingdom was not of this world (see John 18:36), and He came to usher in a new era where the Kingdom of God would break forth into the very place where satan established his throne. When Jesus came from Heaven to the earth, He came as a meek and humble Lamb of God, but make no mistake about it: Jesus, the Alpha and the Omega, the Lord of lords and the King of kings, came to destroy the devil's dominion. Jesus didn't come to coexist with the devil. He came to destroy his works. The Bible says,

> *He who sins is of the devil, for the devil has sinned from the beginning. For this purpose the Son of God was manifested, that He might destroy the works of the devil.* (1 John 3:8)

Jesus came to bring the Kingdom of God upon the earth and to fill all things (see Matt. 4:23; Eph. 4:10)! In short, Jesus came to bring the Kingdom, which can easily be thought of as the *King's dominion*.

When the disciples asked Jesus how to pray, Jesus said,

> *In this manner, therefore, pray: Our Father in heaven, Hallowed be Your name. Your kingdom come. Your will be done On earth as it is in heaven.* (Matt. 6:9–10)

Jesus wasn't just telling His disciples a laundry list of prayer requests. He revealed God's mission to bring His Kingdom to the earth. He said, "Your Kingdom come!" Your will be done on the earth as it is done in Heaven! This was a declaration for God's dominion that is experienced in Heaven to be experienced upon the earth! This was a declaration that Jesus wanted His disciples to get in alignment with His mission to bring Heaven to the earth!

Though many people teach only the Gospel of Jesus Christ is the Good News of salvation, the reality is that the Good News is the coming of the Kingdom of God to the earth. This means that the Gospel of Jesus Christ is more than a message on how to get saved and then "hold on" until Jesus comes back. The Gospel message brings salvation to the individual, but goes further to establish the "King's" Dominion" upon the earth! Jesus was the second Adam who came to save that which was lost and restore all things! His work upon the cross was more than just the payment for our sins; it was also the destruction of the rule and reign of satan!

Look how clear it becomes that Jesus brought the Good News that the Kingdom of God had come! A new rule, a new reign, a new government, and a new King had come!

> *And Jesus went about all Galilee, teaching in their synagogues, preaching the gospel of the kingdom, and healing all kinds of sickness and all kinds of disease among the people.* (Matt. 4:23)

> *Then Jesus went about all the cities and villages, teaching in their synagogues, preaching the gospel of the kingdom, and healing every sickness and every disease among the people.* (Matt. 9:35)

> *And this gospel of the kingdom will be preached in all the world as a witness to all the nations, and then the end will come.* (Matt. 24:14)

> *Now after John was put in prison, Jesus came to Galilee, preaching the gospel of the kingdom of God, and saying, "The time is fulfilled, and the kingdom of God is at hand. Repent, and believe in the gospel."* (Mark 1:14–15)

> *Now after John was put in prison, Jesus came to Galilee, preaching the gospel of the kingdom of God, and saying, "The time is fulfilled, and the kingdom*

of God is at hand. Repent, and believe in the gospel." (Mark 1:14–15)

The Law and the Prophets were proclaimed until John; since that time the gospel of the kingdom of God has been preached, and everyone is forcing his way into it. (Luke 16:16, NASB95)

THE AUTHORITY OF GOD'S WORD

And they feared exceedingly, and said to one another, "Who can this be, that even the wind and the sea obey Him!" (Mark 4:41)

There's an order to our created world that's vitally important to understand. God's Word created our world, and the world didn't create God's Word (see Heb. 11:3). Though this may be common knowledge to many Christians, the understanding of its implications isn't.

If God's Word "framed" or created our world, it has authority in it and authority *over* it! When Jesus Christ was awoken during a storm, the Bible says, *". . . He arose and rebuked the wind, and said to the sea, "Peace, be still!" And the wind ceased and there was a great calm."* (Mark 4:39). Jesus simply spoke to the wind and the sea, because His Word has creative authority over the creation— the wind and the sea. There is no debate, no contention, and no wrestling between the creative Word and the creation. The creation simply bows in obedience.

God and His Word, because they're one, both come from a different Kingdom, and because the King of that Kingdom is in sovereign authority, whatever that King speaks simply is. In Mark 4 as well as many other examples of Jesus demonstrating

His authority over creation, we're seeing the demonstration of the power and authority of God's Kingdom released over His creation!

When Jesus shows up walking upon the water, the disciples in the boat cried out for fear.

> *But immediately Jesus spoke to them, saying, "Be of good cheer! It is I; do not be afraid."* (Matt. 14:27)

Jesus essentially told them to be joyful, because it was Him, and they should not be afraid! When Jesus said, "It is I," it more accurately translated, "I am" (*ego eimi*), leaving off the additional pronoun ("he") (see Matt. 14:27).[1] In other words, God is revealing the nature of His identity and that He is the great "I AM" and His authority reigns above all His creation! What a picture of the Word of God reigning over that which it created! Thus, Jesus' message to the disciples is essentially to be of good courage, for He is the revelation of the "I AM WHO I AM," revealed to Moses in the burning bush in Exodus 3:14.

The disciples didn't yet understand the full nature and identity of Jesus yet, so to see Him walking upon the water would have scared anyone. Nevertheless, Peter being bold and filled with faith said,

> *... "Lord, if it is You, command me to come to You on the water." So He said, "Come." And when Peter had come down out of the boat, he walked on the water to go to Jesus.* (Matt. 14:28–29)

Peter essentially asked Jesus to "command" Him to come. He asked Jesus to put him under the authority of His Word to "come." Jesus met Peter's faith and answered him back with exactly the same word, and said, "come." Peter got out of the boat and literally walked on the water! He walked upon the authority of God's Word which enabled him to walk in the spiritual authority of God's heavenly realm, which reigns over God's natural creation. Then something happened we can probably all relate to. He forgot the awesome revelation that God's Word is in *authority* of over all creation.

> *But when he saw that the wind was boisterous, he was afraid; and beginning to sink he cried out, saying, "Lord, save me!"* (Matt. 14:30)

Peter took his focus off the One whom created the wind and the waves and "saw" the power of that which had been created. Peter, being a fisherman all his life, understood too well the power of the wind and the waves and the danger they represented. His life experience taught him that a human being had no power over such forces and that they were traditionally under the authority of them. Thus, he became afraid. The fact is that in mere moments, a competition of authority took place in Peter's heart between the authority of the Word of God and the authority of the wind and the waves. Of course, no competition took place in the spiritual realm between the Word of God and His creation because God's sovereignty is secure and unchanging. The order of creation has never changed and never will. God's Word is over creation . . . period. Nevertheless, Peter, because of a natural, learned response, believed the power and authority of the wind and the waves were greater than the power and authority of God's Word. The result? He became afraid and sank and needed to cry out to Jesus for Him to save him! He had to call upon the power and authority of Jesus, the Word of God, to once again usurp the natural power of gravity and save him!

And immediately Jesus stretched out His hand and
caught him . . .(Matt. 14:31)

The grace and mercy of God didn't just stretch out His hand to save him. The grace and mercy of God "immediately" stretched out His hand and caught him! Thank you God!

Many of us are quick to talk about how we're in awe of Peter's faith. Let's be real about this. Peter removed himself from a perfectly sound boat in the middle of a storm, which was the only source of natural protection he had. This was a "do" or "die" situation, because once Peter left the boat, it would've quickly drifted away from him and he probably wouldn't have been able to get back in during this time of violent wind and waves. Peter totally committed to this decision to come under the authority of God's Word.

The amazing thing is that Jesus didn't talk about Peter's great faith. He spoke about his "little faith! He spoke about his doubt"!

And immediately Jesus stretched out His hand and
caught him, and said to him, "O you of little faith, why
did you doubt?" And when they got into the boat, the
wind ceased. (Matt. 14:31–32)

To the disciples, it's an amazing thing that Jesus walked on water. To us, it's an amazing thing that Peter got out of the boat and walked on water. To God, however, it's not at all amazing that Jesus or Peter walked upon the water. It's all a matter of perspective. To God, the earth, the water, the wind, the waves, the air, everything was made by Him! He is above the wind and waves! Jesus is the Word of God, and if He can create the sea and all that is in it, it is no big deal for Him to walk upon His creation! In addition, Peter is God's creation and it's therefore no big deal for God's Word to release its authority over Peter to walk on top of the water. Simply put, God has power over all that He creates. The picture of Peter walking on the water is a picture of the authority of God directing one piece of His creation, Peter, to walk on top of another piece of creation, the water! It's all under the authority of God's Word!

This was a powerful lesson for Peter. It taught him that the King and His Word are supreme! As Vernon Law once said, "Experience is a hard teacher because she gives the test first, the lesson afterward". As for us, we need to get the lesson so we can experience the glory realm of God and proverbially walk on water. When Jesus demonstrated His authority over His creation, He demonstrated He was above all their life circumstance. The boat, which represents safety provided by the work of men's hands, was tossed around by the wind and waves. Jesus, which is the revelation of God's Word and power, walked on top of the circumstances completely unshaken.

Jesus demonstrated He was a King from another Kingdom superseding the Kingdom of this natural world. He walked in the realm of His glory, and invited Peter to walk in the realm of God's full government and power we refer to as the Kingdom of God.

THE WORD AND THE KINGDOM OF GOD

Then they were all amazed, so that they questioned among themselves, saying, "What is this? What new doctrine is this? For with authority He commands even the unclean spirits, and they obey Him." (Mark 1:27)

We can never separate the King from His Kingdom. The King of a Kingdom is the highest authority and clearest representation of that Kingdom. As it goes with the King, so it goes with His Kingdom. When the word or edict of a King is released, the will, power, and authority of that Kingdom are released, and there's no other realm this is truer than the Kingdom of God.

When Jesus revealed the Lord's Prayer in Matthew 6, He told us to pray for the Father's Kingdom to come and for His will to be done on earth as it is done in Heaven. How would the Father's Kingdom come? How would His will be done on earth as it's done in Heaven? The answer is the culmination of all that we've been saying! It's through His Word! God's Word is the power of His Kingdom, and it's the release of His will! It's the release of God Himself! When God spoke in Genesis 1:3 for there to be light, His Kingdom of light pierced the kingdom of darkness! When God sent His Word, Jesus Christ, into the world He released His will and overcame the kingdom of darkness!

Of all the things that Jesus could spend His time doing, he focused specifically on three things: teaching the Word, preaching the Word, and releasing His Word in healing. The Word was at the center of all Jesus did, because He was releasing and establishing and expanding the Kingdom of God upon the earth. When Jesus taught the Word of God, He was instructing us on the Kingdom of God. When Jesus preached the Word, He proclaimed the Kingdom of God, and when Jesus healed, He demonstrated the *power* of the Word of God! Jesus is more than a teacher, more than a preacher, and more than a healer! Jesus is the Word who became flesh, and He's the very embodiment of the Word to bring forth the very Kingdom of God itself! He is the carrier and the releaser of the Kingdom of God! Jesus was the expression of God's perfect will in Heaven and now He's God's perfect will upon the earth! Thus, at the heart of the Lord's Prayer in Matthew chapter 6 is the Heavenly cry for Jesus to be released upon the earth because He, in a sense, is Heaven on earth!

> *And Jesus went about all Galilee, teaching in their synagogues, preaching the gospel of the kingdom, and healing all kinds of sickness and all kinds of disease among the people. Then His fame went throughout all Syria; and they brought to Him all sick people who were afflicted with various diseases and torments, and those who were demon-possessed, epileptics, and paralytics; and He healed them.* (Matt. 4:23–24)

Jesus both preached and demonstrated the Good News of the Kingdom. Where He preached the Kingdom, He released the Kingdom! They brought all kinds of sick people to Jesus, and He healed all kinds of sickness and all kinds of disease among the people and He cast out demons from people, because there is no sickness, disease, or demons in Heaven! Jesus brought Heaven to the earth! The Word **brought** Heaven to earth! The Word of God **brings** Heaven to earth! No wonder why the devil hates the Word of God so much! No wonder the first thing the devil did on the earth to attack human beings was to attack the Word of God!

> *Now the serpent was more cunning than any beast of the field which the Lord God had made. And he said to the woman, "Has God indeed said, 'You shall not eat of every tree of the garden'?"* (Gen. 3:1)

As we'll learn more later, satan is afraid of the Word of God because the Word of God is the authority of God, and he has no choice but to submit to it!

Now there was a man in their synagogue with an unclean spirit. And he cried out, saying, "Let us alone! What have we to do with You, Jesus of Nazareth? Did You come to destroy us? I know who You are—the Holy One of God!" But Jesus rebuked him, saying, "Be quiet, and come out of him!" And when the unclean spirit had convulsed him and cried out with a loud voice, he came out of him. Then they were all amazed, so that they questioned among themselves, saying, "What is this? What new doctrine is this? For with authority He commands even the unclean spirits, and they obey Him." And immediately His fame spread throughout all the region around Galilee. (Mark 1:23–28)

The unclean spirit saw Jesus and cried out unveiling the reality that they knew who they were and who Jesus was. They knew they were cursed to be destroyed by Him, and they knew Jesus was the Holy One of God! Truly, there is no confusion between light and dark in the spiritual world! Demons see Jesus and obey Him! They recognize that He is a King from another Kingdom and they must submit because Jesus is a far more powerful King of a greater Kingdom than satan, the king of the world. They must submit to the Word made flesh, because King Jesus is the King of kings and the Kingdom of God reigns over the Kingdom of darkness!

Jesus didn't come to coexist with darkness. He came to displace satan's rule and reign with the Kingdom of God! The Word, the visible glory of God (see Matt. 17:1–8), came to take back the keys of authority given to the devil by the first Adam! God restores, establishes, and expands His Kingdom rule through His Word. Wherever the Word of God is received, so there is God's Kingdom and rule received!

THE KINGDOM OF GOD IN YOUR LIFE

Then the Lord said to Moses, "Make a fiery serpent, and set it on a pole; and it shall be that everyone who is bitten, when he looks at it, shall live." So Moses made a bronze serpent, and put it on a pole; and so it was, if a serpent had bitten anyone, when he looked at the bronze serpent, he lived. (Num. 21:8–9)

The Kingdom of God is not simply an esoteric or philosophical idea. It's the very real and powerful rule and reign of God. It's more than a place and more than just authority. It's more accurately a realm in which the fullness of God's light dwells and darkness has no part. When the Word of God breaks through, the Kingdom of God breaks through, and it creates the environment for the miraculous to happen in your life.

I distinctly remember conducting a three-day healing meeting in Pennsylvania. I received awareness from God that the people shouldn't wait for me to lay hands on them, but could receive God's healing as they heard His Word. I was preaching from the book of Numbers about how God told Moses to make a fiery serpent and that anyone who was bitten could look at the bronze serpent and be healed. I knew that this was a picture of the coming of Jesus Christ (see John 3:14–15), and according to this principle, I knew if the people would receive the healing Word of God, they would see Jesus and receive their healing! Somewhere in the course of the preaching, a woman stood up and declared she was healed. We all glorified God and then I continued preaching. Then, a few moments later, the Pastor of the church declared that his legs were healed! More and more people got touched, and the altars became full of people getting healed!

Healing became easy in that room because the Word of God was received by so many. Thus, the authority of God's Kingdom was able to rest in that place. Sickness and disease were no longer able to function because they are not part of the Kingdom of God!

If you desire to release the power of supernatural blessings, you need to function in the realm of supernatural light. This means you need to "walk on water" in God's Kingdom realm, and you do that by receiving and becoming saturated with Jesus, the revelation of the Word of God.

We are called to receive the Kingdom of God, walk in the Kingdom of God, and be ambassadors of Jesus as we sit with Him in Heavenly places (see Eph. 2:6)! We should not be poor of the things of God's Kingdom because we have the "Word of the Kingdom" (see Matt. 13:19).

Hear the Word of God, receive the Word of God, speak the Word of God, pray the Word of God and let God's Kingdom come and His will be done (see Matt. 6:9–10)!

Do not fear, little flock, for it is your Father's good pleasure to give you the kingdom. (Luke 12:32)

CHAPTER SUMMARY POINTS

1. Jesus Christ brought more than just salvation to individuals. He brought the Kingdom of God to the earth.

2. God sent Jesus Christ, His Son, the Word of God, to the earth as the complete and full representation and ambassador of the Kingdom of Heaven. God's Word is over all creation and has authority over all that's been created. Even the wind and waves obey Jesus because they were created by God's Word.

3. When the Word of the King comes, the power and authority of that Kingdom come. God's Kingdom comes and God's will comes, and Heaven comes to the earth when God's Word is released!

4. If you desire to function in the power of the supernatural blessings, you need to function in the realm of supernatural light. This means you need to "walk on water" in God's Kingdom realm and you do that by receiving and becoming saturated with Jesus, the revelation of the Word of God.

5. We are called to receive the Kingdom of God, walk in the Kingdom of God, and be ambassadors of Jesus as we sit with Him in Heavenly places (see Eph. 2:6)! We should not be poor of the things of God's Kingdom because we have the "Word of the Kingdom" (see Matt. 13:19).

QUESTIONS FOR REFLECTION

1. What is the difference between receiving the blessings of individual salvation and receiving the Kingdom of God?

2. In what ways have I come under, or believed in, the authority of natural circumstances over the authority of God's Word?

3. Have you received the Word of God from God or people? In other words, have you received the Word of God in a way that reflects the sovereign power of God Almighty rather than the opinion of people?

4. How can you increase the amount of God's Word in your life so you become saturated with the will, desire, and Kingdom of God?

5. Have you accepted defeat and lack concerning things in your life rather than excitement that comes from understanding

the blessings of God's Kingdom in your life? If yes, are you willing to repent and receive the full blessings of the Gospel of Jesus Christ by accepting *every* Word that proceeds from the mouth of God? (See Matthew 4:4.)

PRAYER

Father, I declare in the Name of Jesus Christ that I will walk in the fullness of all that You have provided me in Jesus! I receive Your Word as the Word of the Alpha and the Omega and the beginning and the end, and the Lord of lords and the King of kings. I declare that I shall submit fully and entirely to Your holy Word so as to allow You to release Your Kingdom in my life and family and church! I declare that I shall recognize that Your Word is sovereign over all other natural circumstances and I shall have confidence in Your Word. I declare I shall believe Your Word over the testimony of every other thing! I receive the Word of Your Kingdom, and I boldly pray . . . Our Father in Heaven, Hallowed be Your name. Your Kingdom come. Your will be done On earth as it is in Heaven. Give us this day our daily bread. And forgive us our debts, As we forgive our debtors. And do not lead us into temptation, But deliver us from the evil one. For Yours is the Kingdom and the power and the glory forever. Amen."

ENDNOTE

[1]John D. Barry, Michael Grigoni, Michael S. Heiser, Miles Custis, Douglas Mangum, and Matthew M. Whitehead, *Faithlife Study Bible* (Bellingham, WA: Logos Bible Software, 2012).

Chapter 7

THE DEVIL'S DEFEAT

THE SPIRIT, THE WORD, AND MINISTRY

Then Jesus, being filled with the Holy Spirit, returned from the Jordan and was led by the Spirit into the wilderness, (Luke 4:1)

Jesus Christ had just been baptized by John the Baptist in the Jordan River, and the Heavens were opened and the Spirit of God descended in bodily form upon Jesus (see Luke 3:21–22). Amazingly, the next thing Jesus did was head into the desert. He did this, the Bible said, because the Holy Spirit led Him to go. The Gospel of Matthew in Chapter 4, Verse 1, tells us God wanted His Son to be tempted by the devil! This has puzzled many Christians, and an entire book could be written on the subject as to the deep meaning behind this, but for our purposes, let's unpack at least one key part of God's awesome plan.

When Jesus Christ was baptized and the Holy Spirit descended upon Him, God was showing a mighty picture of Jesus' work in the Gospel. Jesus Christ is God, and He was and is and always will be perfect, blameless, and without sin. He had no need to be forgiven, and never needed to be born again as a sinner, because He never sinned. In addition, Jesus, being God, didn't need to be anointed because He was already fully God. However, Jesus did all these things for righteousness sake (see Matt. 3:15) because He assumed our position and walked through everything we as sinners would walk through. Jesus Christ is the Word of God "made flesh", and all that had been prophesied about Him by the law and the prophets had to come to pass.

Thus, we see the Father open the Heavens and send the Holy Spirit upon Him (see Matthew 3:16). What a powerful demonstration of Father God affirming His Son's identity and the Holy Spirit anointing Him, the Word of God, in preparation for ministry! It's confirmation that the Word of God had been sent into the world and anointed to accomplish God's mission.

THE DEVIL ATTACKS

Then Jesus was led up by the Spirit into the wilderness to be tempted by the devil. And when He had fasted forty days and forty nights, afterward He was hungry. Now when the tempter came to Him, he said, "If You are the Son of God, command that these stones become bread" (Matt. 4:1–3).

The Holy Spirit sent Jesus into the wilderness because it represents the destruction of sin in the Garden of Eden and the place the devil was first announced to be. Satan was called more cunning than any "beast of the field" (see Gen. 3:1). Thus, Jesus went into the "field" to deal with the beast who dwelt there. In the book of Genesis, the one in the desert overcame those in the Garden. In the Gospels, the One from Heaven went to overcome the one in the wilderness. Thus, the first ministry assignment the Holy Spirit sent Jesus on wasn't to the poor, to the sick, to the hurting, to sinners who needed grace, to the Jewish people who were looking for His coming or even to a human being. The first place the Holy Spirit sent Jesus was into the wilderness to deal with the king of the world, the devil. The Word of God was sent into the wilderness to deal with our adversary!

Jesus being born King didn't need to inherit power or authority. He was already imbued with power from on high in the Kingdom of Heaven. Thus, when Jesus Christ was sent into the wilderness, He was a superior King from the Kingdom of Heaven sent to deal with a lessor king in the kingdom of the world. I love the fact that when the Bible says in Matthew 4 that the tempter "came" to Jesus he was only reacting to God's plan. God was the One who initiated the move. God was the aggressor in this situation. Jesus wasn't reacting to the devil's temptation in a passive way, but rather was sent so He could deal with the tempter. God set up the devil for a major defeat—a defeat the devil has never forgotten even to this very day!When Jesus was sent into the wilderness, though He was 100 percent God, He walked in the likeness of man. So when the Bible tells us Jesus fasted 40 days and 40 nights and was hungry afterward, we have to understand that He was *hungry*! His body, His mind, and His whole being would've been fatigued, filled with aches, and over all incredibly weak. It was a time Jesus suffered in a barren place with no provision.

Characteristic of the devil, he waited until Jesus was in the weakest state at the end of His fast, and he came with three temptations designed to capitalize on the weakness of the flesh.

First, satan tempted Jesus in the area of physical hunger. He said,

Now when the tempter came to Him, he said, "If You are the Son of God, command that these stones become bread." (Matt. 4:3)

This temptation is the most basic of all temptations, and impacts physical desire rooted in the **physical body.**

Second, satan tempted Jesus to prove His identity.

Then the devil took Him up into the holy city, set Him on the pinnacle of the temple, and said to Him, "If You are the Son of God, throw Yourself down. For it is written: 'He shall give His angels charge over you,' and, "In their hands they shall bear you up, Lest you dash your foot against a stone.'" (Matt. 4:5–6)

The "holy city" refers to Jerusalem, and the pinnacle of the temple was approximately 300 feet above the floor of the Kidron Valley.[1] The devil attempted to manipulate Jesus' heart and mind by twisting the Scriptures. He wanted Jesus to misapply God's Word. It was a temptation targeted at His soul, which comprises a person's mind, will, and emotions.

The final and third temptation focused upon Jesus' heart of worship.

Again, the devil took Him up on an exceedingly high mountain, and showed Him all the kingdoms of the world and their glory. And he said to Him, "All these things I will give You if You will fall down and worship me" (Matt. 4:8–9).

The devil showed Him all the kingdoms of the world and their glory. This temptation attacked the very core of fallen nature, which craves and lusts after power and selfish ambition.

Satan presented an opportunity for Jesus to exchange His selfless love for the love of self. The devil was able to show and offer the kingdoms of the world and their glory because they were delivered to him by Adam in the Garden of Eden! All that had been cursed was put under the devil's authority. No blessed thing was put under the devil's authority, only that which had been cursed through the curse of the law of sin and death.

Each time the devil tested Jesus, it was as if he upped the stakes moving from tempting the needs of His Body to the issues of His soul to the desires of His heart. This is exactly how the devil attacks all human beings and successfully conquered every person since Adam and Eve. Truly the devil deployed the very same tactics against Jesus hoping He would bend His knee in disobedience to God. However, the devil wasn't dealing with just a human being. He was dealing with Jesus, the "second Adam," (see 1 Cor. 15:45) who, though was in likeness of a man, was the perfect and sinless King of kings! Because Jesus never sinned, He was not under the curse and therefore, not under the devil's authority. For the first time ever, the devil had no authority over someone walking in the flesh! The lesser "king of the world" picked a fight with the far greater King of Heaven! The Alpha and the Omega, the beginning and the end!

THE DEVIL ENCOUNTERED GOD'S WORD

But He answered and said, "It is written..." (Matt. 4:4)

When the Spirit of God led Jesus into the wilderness, He sent the Word of God into the wilderness! Though His physical body was weakened because of His 40-day fast, His spiritual body, the Word of God, remained strong. Jesus was more than met the eye, and satan met exactly what God the Father wanted him to meet. He met His Word!

Whenever the devil attempted to bring Jesus under his rule through temptation, Jesus, the incarnate form of the Word, spoke the written form of the Word of God. In other words, he quoted the Scripture! He said, "It is written."

When the devil tempted Jesus to eat bread, he tempted Jesus to live, rely upon, and find a source of life and strength from that which is natural. Jesus responded with God's Word and quoted Deuteronomy 8:3, an allusion to the fact that God supplied manna from heaven to the Israelites and a direct allusion that the true "Bread of Life" from heaven had arrived! Once Jesus spoke declaring that a person's source of life comes from every Word that proceeds from the mouth of God, the devil left that tempation. He was defeated. Nothing more needed to happen. The Word of God stopped him dead in his tracks. He could only try to tempt Jesus in another area.

When the devil tempted Jesus to throw Himself down from the temple peak, Jesus quoted Deuteronomy 6:16! Once again, the incarnate form of the Word spoke the written form of the Word and overcame the enemy!

Finally, when the devil offered Jesus all the kingdoms of the world if He would worship Him, Jesus Christ quoted the Word of God in Deuteronomy 6:13! Once again the incarnate form of the Word spoke the written form of the Word and overcame the devil! In response to the devil's last temptation Jesus commanded satan to get behind Him! (see Matt. 4:10) What a powerful demonstration of the Word of God telling the devil to get behind Him! All that has been revealed, spoken, prophesied, and written concerning the Father's heart, will, and desire are in Jesus. Every covenant promise is revealed as "yes" in Jesus Christ. The testimony of the spirit of prophecy commanded the devil to get behind Him.

Right now, the Word of God speaks the same thing! The covenant promises speak the same thing! You can speak and release that which God demonstrated through His Son, Jesus, in the wilderness. You can overcome the devil in the wilderness by believing and releasing the Word of God! In fact, when Jesus fasted for 40 days and nights and released the Word of God against the devil, He wasn't operating in His deity. He was operating in His humanity. It's a picture of what a born-again, baptized, spirit-filled, word-filled believer looks like when they resist the king of this world with the Word of God! Jesus Christ was demonstrating what it looked like to walk in the provision we've been given. We've been given the Word of God! We've been given the Holy Spirit! We have the same provision! Without question Jesus Christ demonstrated what victory looks like, and how to achieve it!

We need to have such a command of God's Word that when the devil speaks to us, he'll hear nothing but God's Word spoken back to him. Jesus may have walked as a man, but He responded to temptation like God! When the devil squeezed Jesus, the Word of God came out. When the devil squeezes us, the Word of God should come forth just the same! However, when was the last time any of us memorized the book of Deuteronomy and understood its application like Jesus? We definitely need more of the Word of God to resist the devil in our lives! Jesus didn't just quote a Bible verse or go through a religious action of confessing Scripture. He was in fact one with the Word because He and the Word are one!

His supernatural nature broke through and defeated the devil at every turn. In fact, Jesus had to "lay down his life" because the devil lacked the authority to take it. He couldn't overcome the Word of God; he couldn't overcome God!

Truly, He who is in us is greater than he who is in the world (see 1 John 4:4)! The Word of God should be released from us and put every ounce of the devil's authority into subjection to it. Jesus Christ said, "Get behind Me satan!" The Word said, "Get behind me satan!" We should boldly command, "Get behind me satan!"

THE DEVIL SEES HIS DEFEAT!

Put on the whole armor of God, that you may be able to stand against the wiles of the devil. (Eph. 6:11)

For thousands upon thousands of years the devil never ever experienced defeat in front of flesh. All had succumbed to temptation. All had bowed their knees to him. All succumbed to him. The only one to ever successfully resist his temptation was Jesus Christ! Although satan threw all he at Jesus, he couldn't win. He couldn't manipulate Him; he couldn't cause Jesus to bend His knee to Him. At every temptation, Jesus Christ shut satan down fast and hard, because satan encountered more than flesh and blood. He encountered the Word of God! Satan clearly understands through personal experience that he cannot overcome the Word of God. **When the devil sees the Word of God, he sees his defeat!**

Paul's letter to the Ephesians tells us that we are to stand strong in the power and might of the Lord Jesus. That we do not wrestle against flesh and blood, but against spiritual entities. He goes on to urge the Christians to "put on the whole armor of God" that they will be able to stand against the things the devil is doing. He goes on to metaphorically describe pieces of armor that all refer to the Word of God. In fact, a close study of the armor of God reveals that he is telling the Christians to put on Jesus Christ! In other words, they needed to be covered by the Word of God!

When the devil sees a believer covered with the armor of God, he sees them covered with Jesus Christ. When he sees them covered with Jesus Christ, he sees them covered with the Word of God and that causes him to see only one thing: his defeat!

This is why every Christian must be fully grounded in the Word of God and nothing less. The only thing that really brings victory over the devil is that which is rooted and grounded and springs forth from the Word of God! We can sing, shout, stomp our feet, roll around on the floor, wave our hands, immerse ourselves in anointing oil, pray and fast for years, attend conferences, read books, serve the homeless, yet never make any significant headway against the work of the wiles of the devil in our lives.

Until a believer's heart is rooted and grounded and established in the Word of God, they are on shaky ground. Their faith will be fragile, their worship will be shallow, and their capacity to receive new revelation and produce fruit will all be compromised. To deeply understand that the Word of God is the revelation and release of God is to understand that anything that becomes disconnected from the Word of God is to become disconnected from God.

Too many people begin their walk in the Word of God and slowly drift away. It may take weeks, months, or years, but the devil is determined to get us away from the Word of God as much as he can. Each of us must guard ourselves from things that seem good, look good, sound good, but are not from God's Word. It's a discipline that gets developed over time, but we must become trained to cling to and remain tethered to the Word of God.

This is the key to your success against the enemy: become so filled with God's Word that every time the devil comes to you and presses against you, he finds himself pressing against the Word of God. The scariest thing in the world to the devil is not the people on stages and platforms who often get world-based fame, but it's the person in their prayer closet on their knees reading, receiving, believing, and acting upon the Word of God.

When a person is consumed with the Word of God, they are equipped and well able to overcome all the wiles of the devil! They hold the Word, they believe the Word, they pray the Word, they speak the Word, and they become one with the Word of God. They resist the devil with the Word, and he gets shut down just as he did with Jesus in the wilderness.

THE DEVIL'S ATTEMPT TO DISCONNECT US

. . . For this purpose the Son of God was manifested, that He might destroy the works of the devil." (1 John 3:8)

The Son of God came to destroy the works of the devil. In other words, the Word of God came to destroy the works of the devil. When the Word of God is truly applied with faith, nothing in all creation is possible except for the devil to be defeated by it. The devil knows this better than anyone, and this is why he does all he can to disconnect us from God's Word.

Said plainly, the devil is afraid of the Word of God more than anything in all creation! The devil hates the Word of God, and he hates it with a passion impossible to express. He despises it to such a degree that he wants it removed from every home, from every school, from the media, from our government, from our churches, and from the hearts and minds of believers. We are arguably in an era like no other in our country. Never before has the Word of God been so disdained in government, politics, business, education, the media, and the like. Core Christian values of faith and family are openly criticized, Christians are targeted with acts of terror with very little, if any, recognition from the United States government, and the presence of the Ten Commandments on government property is now considered offensive by many.

In two landmark court decisions, *Engel v. Vitale* (1962) and *Abington School District v. Schempp* (1963), the United States Supreme Court established the current prohibition on state-sponsored prayer in schools. These monumental decisions set a course to remove the presence of God from schools, and its ramifications have been significant.

The Specialty Research Associates, under the direction of David Barton, released a report entitled *America: To Pray or Not To Pray*. The following statics are only a few examples of the effect of removing God from our schools.

IMPACT ON YOUNG PEOPLE

1. For 15 years before 1963, pregnancies in girls aged 15 through 19 years had been no more than 15 per 1,000. After 1963, pregnancies increased 187 percent in the next 15 years.

2. For younger girls, aged 10–14 years, pregnancies since 1963 are up 553 percent.

3. Before 1963, sexually transmitted diseases among students were 400 per 100,000. Since 1963, they were up 226 percent in the next 12 years.

IMPACT ON THE FAMILY

1. Before 1963, divorce rates had been declining for 15 years. After 1963, divorces increased 300 percent *each year* for the next 15 years.

2. Since 1963, unmarried people living together are up 353 percent.

3. Since 1963, single-parent families are up 140 percent.

4. Since 1963, single-parent families with children are up 160 percent.

IMPACT ON EDUCATION

1. The educational standard of measure has been the SAT scores. SAT scores had been steady for many years before 1963. From 1963, they rapidly declined for 18 consecutive years, even though the same test has been used since 1941.

2. In 1974–1975, the rate of decline of the SAT scores decreased, even though they continued to decline. That was when there was an explosion of private religious schools. There were only 1,000 Christian schools in 1965. Between 1974 and 1984, they increased to 32,000.

   a. In checking with the SAT Board, it was found that indeed the SAT scores for private schools were nearly 100 points higher than public schools.

b. In fact, the scores were at the point where the public schools had been before their decline started in 1963 when prayer and Bible reading/instruction was removed from the schools.

c. The scores in the public schools were still declining.

3. Of the nation's top academic scholars, three times as many come from private religious schools, which operate on one-third the funds, as do the public schools.

IMPACT ON THE NATION

1. Since 1963, violent crime has increased 544 percent.

2. Illegal drugs have become an enormous and uncontrollable problem.

3. The nation has been deprived of an estimated 30 million citizens through legal abortions just since 1973.

God sent Jesus, the Word, to the earth to save and heal and deliver us from all our destructions. (See Psalm 107:20; John 3:16, Isa. 53:4–5; 1 John 3:8.) The devil is not supposed to cast out the Word of God from our lives. The Word of God is supposed to cast out the devil! All across the world, the devil over a period of many generations has tried, and is trying to remove the Word of God from the face of the earth. Whether he was lying about it in the Garden of Eden (see Gen. 3:4), killing the prophets in the Old Testament, trying to destroy the Word of God during the early years of church history, attempting to remove the Word of God from our culture, or doing all he can do to presently remove the pure, unadulterated preaching of the Word in God's Church, he is after one thing: the removal of God's Word. Jesus even warned the wayward person about the work of demons to steal the Word of God out of their hearts!

> *And these are the ones by the wayside where the word is sown. When they hear, Satan comes immediately and takes away the word that was sown in their hearts.* (Mark 4:15)

The issues are so much deeper than political or religious freedom. **When the devil is attempting to remove the Word of God from society, he's trying to remove the light of the world from the earth, the salvation of God from the lost, the power of God from the hurting, the Kingdom of God from society, and the breath of Heaven from earth. He's literally trying to remove the Revelation and testimony of Jesus Christ from the earth. The thief who comes only to kill, steal, and to destroy tries to bring a false reality to people to make it seem as if Jesus Christ never came, or at minimum never accomplished anything in His suffering, death, burial, and resurrection.**

The devil will persistently do all he can to prevent people from reading the Word of God, receiving the Word of God, understanding the Word of God, and most of all applying the Word of God to our lives. Martin Luther, a major figure in the Protestant Reformation, said, "All the cunning of the devil is exercised in trying to tear us away from the Word."

Have you ever attempted to read the Word of God at night? You've had a long day at work, you ate a nice dinner, and then decide to dig into the Word of God. You begin reading and about 5 minutes later you feel a tremendous sleepiness come over you. You begin thinking how tired you are, but press in a little bit further. In a short while, you feel the heaviness on your eye lids and begin to fall asleep.

Now let's contrast this to what happens when we don't open the word of God, but watch television or spend time with friends. We somehow don't get as tired, and we're able to continue with a lot of energy. It may not seem like it at first, but this very common occurrence is a spiritual attack. It's not just that the Word of God is boring, or that you're disinterested in what you're reading. It's the devil trying to block you from reading the Word of God.

What about the frequent interruptions that come when you try to read the Word of God? Have you noticed the phone will ring right when you begin reading the Bible, or you begin thinking about the million things that you need to do? Many jokingly confess that they'll sit down to read the Word of God and begin thinking about the fact that there's dust behind the corner curio and feel an urge to clean it! This may sound comical, but the reality is that the devil is trying to distract us with non-urgent and unimportant things to keep us from the power of God's Word.

It makes perfect sense that the devil, the adversary of men, would do all he can to remove the Word of God, which has been sent to heal and deliver us from our destructions. He's trying to remove the very thing that brings him defeat! Do not be deceived; every time we attempt to receive the light, the thief is seeking to kill, steal, and destroy us.

A Day of Freedom

It was a beautiful service where the presence of God sweetly graced us. I was ministering at a well-known Christian-based substance abuse program in the New York area. The men and women worshipped God with an authentic heart grateful and reliant upon God for the help they were receiving. Some were in the program for a while becoming established in their faith and sobriety; others were brand new to the program still wondering whether this "Christian" thing was going to actually work.

As I shared the Good News of Jesus Christ, I focused upon the reality that God makes us new creations when we receive Jesus as our Lord and Savior. I also shared the blessing and freedom that comes to us when we receive God's gift! Many prayed to receive the Lord Jesus Christ as their Lord and Savior, and the Lord blessed many during our time of prayer at the altar.

I thought the service was finished, but I was wrong. One of the faculty members led a severely oppressed woman up the center aisle of the sanctuary, and it was clear this woman needed deliverance.

When she came about 6 feet away from me, she began to resist coming any closer. They brought her yet closer, and she seemed to cower in fear and became unable to speak. It was as if her throat was closing and she couldn't even get any sound out. I knew it was a manifestation of demons inside of her. They were not at all afraid of me, but they were afraid of Jesus Christ in me. They were afraid of the Word of God living inside me! The darkness within her knew their time of oppressing her had come to an end. They knew their rule and reign over her was finished. They already saw their defeat! This very thing happened in Jesus' day when he came to the country of the Gadarenes (see Mark 5:1–8). The demons who bound a man saw Jesus from afar and said,

> . . ."What have I to do with You, Jesus, Son of the Most High God? I implore You by God that You do not torment me." (Mark 5:6–7)

When the devil and his demons see the Word of God, they see their defeat! We prayed with her, and she received the Gospel of

Jesus Christ. As I began ministering the provision of the Gospel of Jesus Christ and spoke the Word of God over her, she became extremely weak, falling to the floor, shaking, and began renouncing all agreement with satan. She asked God to forgive, heal, and set her free. This was the Word of God in action! I commanded the demons to depart from her in the Name of Jesus Christ exactly as the Word of God teaches (see Luke 10:17; Mark 16:17; Matt. 10:1; Acts 3:16). We did what James speaks about in his letter. He said, *"Therefore submit to God. Resist the devil and he will flee from you."* (James 4:7). We submitted to God, resisted the devil, and she became completely free. A short while after, I learned the woman was once again of a sound mind, released from the program, and went home to her family praising God!

From this moment, make the decision to daily abide in the Word of God. Refuse to allow the devil to disconnect you from it! Realize and understand that a schedule that is too busy to dwell in God's Word is a schedule with the devil's hand in it. Remember that when the devil sees the Word of God, he sees the glory and light of God (see John 1:14; 8:12), and he can't overcome the light of the world! (See John 1:5.) Your firm decision to follow the Word of God is the same as making your decision to follow Jesus. Follow Him with all your heart, with all your mind, and with all your strength, and you will never walk in darkness, but will have the light of life!

> *Then Jesus spoke to them again, saying, "I am the light of the world. He who follows Me shall not walk in darkness, but have the light of life."* (John 8:12)

It doesn't matter how long you've suffered, or how bad things have gotten, the Word of God will produce the miracles you've been waiting for in your life! It's impossible for it to fail! It's God's

Word and God can't fail! It's Unleashing Heaven's Breath, Heaven's truth, and Heaven's power! God's record of overcoming the devil and his work says, "UNDEFEATED"! Get so connected to God's Word that you'll become so filled with its revelation, power, and glory that the devil becomes overwhelmed with defeat and flees! It will produce the lifetime of freedom Jesus died to give us!

CHAPTER SUMMARY POINTS

1. When Jesus was baptized in the Jordan River, He was fulfilling God's plan to pave the way for us to walk in salvation. It was a powerful picture of the Father affirming His Son and the Holy Spirit anointing the Word of God in preparation for ministry!

2. The Holy Spirit sent Jesus into the wilderness because it represents the destruction of sin in the Garden of Eden and the place the devil was first announced to be. Satan was called more cunning than any "beast of the field" (see Gen. 3:1).

3. The first ministry assignment the Holy Spirit sent Jesus on wasn't to the poor, to the sick, to the hurting, to sinners who needed grace, to the Jewish people who were looking for His coming or even to a human being. The first place the Holy Spirit sent Jesus was into the wilderness to deal with the king of the world, the devil. The Word of God was sent into the wilderness to deal with our adversary!

4. The power of God is released when the Word of God is spoken. Whenever the devil attempted to bring Jesus under his rule through temptation, Jesus, the incarnate Word, spoke the written form of the Word of God. In other words, he quoted the Scripture! He said, "It is written."

5. At every temptation, Jesus Christ shut satan down fast and hard because satan encountered more than flesh and blood. He encountered the Word of God! Satan clearly understands through personal experience that he cannot overcome the Word of God. When the devil sees the Word of God, he sees his defeat!

6. When the devil is attempting to remove the Word of God from society, he's trying to remove the light of the world from the earth, the salvation of God from the lost, the power of God from the hurting, the Kingdom of God from society, and the breath of Heaven from earth. He's literally trying to remove the revelation and testimony of Jesus Christ from the earth. The thief who comes only to kill, steal, and to destroy tries to bring a false reality to people to make it seem as if Jesus Christ never came, or at minimum never accomplished anything in His suffering, death, burial, and resurrection.

7. It doesn't at all matter how long you've suffered, or how bad things have gotten, the Word of God will produce the miracles you've been waiting for! It's impossible for it to fail! Get so connected to God's Word that you'll become so filled with its revelation, power, and glory that the devil becomes overwhelmed with defeat and flees! It will be your day and lifetime of freedom!

QUESTIONS FOR REFLECTION

1. Think about the most frequent temptations of the enemy in your life. Which temptations are focused on your physical needs? On the needs of your soul? On your spiritual needs?

2. Jesus quoted the Word of God to defeat the devil. What Scriptures can you begin quoting to the devil to overcome

him? Begin believing and speaking them today and shut him down!

3. In what ways can you ensure the devil will never disconnect you from the Word of God? Put your battle plan together of how you'll stay connected to God's Word so you will overcome the devil at every turn!

PRAYER

*Father, I thank You Jesus went in the wilderness to overcome the devil's temptation on my behalf! Thank you for revealing to us how to overcome the devil! I confess I've gotten disconnected from Your Word at times, and I repent. Help me to put Your Word first in my life so I'll stand strong against all the wiles of the devil. Establish me in the **miracle-power** of Your Word. I declare today that I will walk in a new level of victory over temptation, sin, and doubt! I declare my weapons are not natural but supernatural and mighty to pull the enemy down! I cast away every temptation and bring every thought into captivity to the obedience of Christ! I submit to You and Your Word Jesus! Release its power through me so I walk in Your supernatural power! I ask this in the Name of Jesus Christ! Amen!*

ENDNOTE

[1] Crossway Bibles, *The ESV Study Bible* (Wheaton, IL: Crossway Bibles, 2008), 1825.

Chapter 8

RECEIVING HEAVEN'S BREATH

THE NEED TO RECEIVE

Now the serpent was more cunning than any beast of the field which the Lord God had made. And he said to the woman, "Has God indeed said, 'You shall not eat of every tree of the garden'?" And the woman said to the serpent, "We may eat the fruit of the trees of the garden; but of the fruit of the tree which is in the midst of the garden, God has said, 'You shall not eat it, nor shall you touch it, lest you die.'" Then the serpent said to the woman, "You will not surely die." (Gen. 3:1–4)

The revelation that the devil sees his defeat when he sees the Word of God is awesome, and it has the power to completely and radically transform your relationship and hunger for God's Word. However, if we don't understand the keys of connecting and releasing the Word of God, we'll be in danger of living without its power. As mentioned earlier, the devil works violently to disconnect us from God's Word, and does all he can to place obstacles between us and Unleashing Heaven's Breath, which is the same as placing obstacles between us and God Himself! Consequently, we must be aware of the devil's schemes, and shut them down at every attempt.

The first and most foundational key of releasing the supernatural power of God's Word is to simply receive, believe, and act upon it. Thus, at the epicenter of the devil's strategy to prevent the supernatural power of God's Word from being released in our lives is to try to get the Word of God from ever being received, believed, and acted upon. It's simple, but nevertheless major.

The very first temptation recorded in the Bible recounts the devil's plot to separate mankind from God by creating enmity with God's Word. The devil asked one question which was *"Has God indeed said . . ."* (Gen. 3:1–3). Of all the things that could have been said and done, the one thing the devil knew to attack was mankind's reception of the Word of God! Though Eve knew God's command and repeated it back to the devil, the devil launched a counterattack and said, "You will not surely die." After the devil brings God's Word into question, he then casts doubt and confusion with it through carefully architected lies.

The fate of the entire earth, and all that were in it, rested upon how Adam and Eve would receive, believe, and act upon God's spoken Word. Sadly, we know they willfully rejected God's Word, believed the devil, and acted upon his lie. The result was worldwide destruction through the curse of sin and death—a curse that's still operating today. We need to grasp the gravity of the reality that all pain, suffering, sickness, disease, and every other evil thing resulted because mankind responded to God's Word improperly!

The devil didn't overcome Adam and Eve because he was stronger. Adam was delegated God's authority to have dominion over every creeping thing on the earth including the "beast of the field"! (See Genesis 1:24-26.) The only reason the devil overcame Adam and usurped his authority was because mankind chose to listen to the wrong voice. They listened to the wrong word!

The clearest way I imagine this is to think about a terrible bully who desires to pick on a small child. Every time the child and the dad are together, the bully can't attack because he'd have to deal with the child's big, strong dad. Thus, the bully will do all he can to lure the child away from the covering and protection of the dad so he can easily attack. In the same way, the devil can't overcome us when Abba's Word covers and protects us. Thus, he deploys every trick in the book to cause us to willfully walk out from under God's protective, life-giving Word, and he then moves in to try to devour the children of God.

If we consider the state of things closely, we'll quickly realize that the devil isn't very creative, and is deploying the same strategy today in every nation! The devil knows he can't overcome the Word of God because it's the agent of God's authority upon the earth. Thus, he does all he can to win our agreement and cooperation to willfully walk away out from under God's Word.

It's taken generations to happen in America, but the devil has made significant inroads in our society to question, doubt, and even hold a disdain for the things of the Word of God. Though most people say they honor or believe the Word of God, the reality is that most only offer God lip service, and their hearts are far from Him (see Matt. 15:8). In many ways, our current generation is more skeptical about the Bible than any other has ever been. Let's look at the statistics.

- Between 1815 and 1975, it was estimated there were 5 billion Bibles printed.

- More than 168,000 Bibles are sold or given to others in the United States each day.

- Twenty million Bibles are sold each year in the United States. More than double the amount sold annually in the 1950s.

- The Gideon's International distributed 59,460,000 Bibles worldwide last year. That's more than 100 Bibles per minute.

- The average American Christian owns nine Bibles and wants to purchase more. For this reason, the Bible is actually excluded from book bestsellers lists because it would always be on top.[1]

Clearly the problem isn't a lack of Bibles. The problem is how it's received! At the time of the writing of this book, skepticism of the Bible in America is strongly trending upward. The number of people who are skeptical, or agnostic toward the Bible, defined as those who believe the Bible is "just another book of teaching written by man that contains stories and advice," has nearly doubled in just three years, and this trend is believed to be on the rise for years to come. Of the 88 percent of households that own a Bible, only 37 percent report reading the Bible once a week or more, and only 33 percent of millennials believe the Bible has too little influence in society.[2]

The point is that people have more Bibles than ever, but too few have clear revelation of it. When only 37 percent of the people who own a Bible actually crack it open once a week, it means they don't understand the power and importance of it. We may say we believe the Word of God, but we really don't understand the magnitude of miracles the Word of God is ready to release.

It's as if we have eyes, but don't see, and we have ears, but don't hear. Jesus said,

> *For the hearts of this people have grown dull. Their ears are hard of hearing, And their eyes they have closed, Lest they should see with their eyes and hear with their ears, Lest they should understand with their hearts and turn, So that I should heal them.'* (Matt. 13:15)

God is so ready to reveal Himself, but our culture is so much more familiar with doubt-building arguments than with authentic faith-building experiences. There are thousands of world religions in existence, and people wonder whose faith teaching is the "right" one, or if "absolute truth" even exists. Traditional values are slipping faster than ever, and popular social opinion has become a driving force behind many personal belief systems. Our postmodern world has become estranged from the idea that a book containing ancient writings could indeed hold the answers to our modern-day problems. Even many Christians believe the Bible can't be fully trusted, fully understood, or practically lived in modern society.

As a Senior Pastor, Bible School Professor, and traveling minister among churches and marketplace leaders, **I've come to understand the root to most barriers to a person's breakthrough is not a lack of biblical information, although this greatly exists, but rather a lack of receiving the true nature of the Word of God as the perfect revelation of God's will and character.**

If a person believes the Bible is authored by God, they'll consider the source infallible, trustworthy, and perfect in every way. They'll be able to apply it with great confidence and reap indescribable benefit. If they think it's written by men, filled with faulty opinions and nice, encouraging "stories," they will be hard pressed to receive much. It really doesn't matter how much information is given. It matters how much revelation is released and applied in our everyday lives.

How we receive and relate to the Word of God impacts our destiny not only upon the earth, but also for all eternity! It's a strong statement, but absolutely true. No matter how much grace, how much blessing, and how much revelation God desires to impart to us, it will be hindered if we don't receive it properly. Even our very salvation depends on how we receive the Word of God! Let's briefly look at the danger of not receiving God's Word.

> *He who despises the word will be destroyed, But he who fears the commandment will be rewarded.* (Prov. 13:13)

> *For whoever is ashamed of Me and My words, of him the Son of Man will be ashamed when He comes in His own glory, and in His Father's, and of the holy angels.* (Luke 9:26)

> *Therefore, as the fire devours the stubble, And the flame consumes the chaff, So their root will be as rottenness, And their blossom will ascend like dust; Because they have rejected the law of the Lord of hosts, And despised the word of the Holy One of Israel.* (Isa. 5:24)

> *He who is of God hears God's words; therefore you do not hear, because you are not of God."* (John 8:47)

> *He who rejects Me, and does not receive My words, has that which judges him—the word that I have spoken will judge him in the last day.* (John 12:48)

Let's now briefly look at the examples of those receiving God's Word.

> *Therefore lay aside all filthiness and overflow of wickedness, and receive with meekness the implanted word, which is able to save your souls.* (James 1:21)

> *Then those who gladly received his word were baptized; and that day about three thousand souls were added to them.* (Acts 2:41)

> *Now the apostles and brethren who were in Judea heard that the Gentiles had also received the word of God.* (Acts 11:1)

> *These were more fair-minded than those in Thessalonica, in that they received the word with all readiness, and searched the Scriptures daily to find out whether these things were so.* (Acts 17:11)

> *For this reason we also thank God without ceasing, because when you received the word of God which you heard from us, you welcomed it not as the word of men, but as it is in truth, the word of God, which also effectively works in you who believe.* (1 Thess. 2:13)

> *As for God, His way is perfect; The word of the Lord is proven; He is a shield to all who trust in Him.* (Ps. 18:30)

God is actively seeking those who will partner with His work upon the earth, and He's given His Word as His plumb line by which all partnering with God should occur. Without question, the ultimate state of our jobs, families, churches, and very lives all hinge upon how we respond to God's Word! When our beliefs about the Bible become aligned with Heaven, the abundant grace and power of God is released! Not like a weak river, but like an exploding geyser of glory that consumes everything around it!

The Word of God is the revelation of what Christianity could and should be. Nevertheless, this issue of how Christians really view the Bible and what we really think about it is amazingly and frequently overlooked. We may hear preaching and teaching tell us to "stand" on the "Word" or "believe" the Word, or put our "trust" in the Word, but have we received the Word of God in a way that enables us to do these very important things? Do we trust it enough to "stand" upon it in when it really matters? Do we know why we can "believe" it because of more than scientific or archeological data? Have we spiritually encountered God's Word in such a way that enables us to live through Jesus, or better yet, allow Jesus to live through us? (See Galatians 2:20.) Have we pierced through simple mental agreement with teaching, and launched into a revelatory understanding of the supernatural power of God's Word where miracles take place and God's will in Heaven breaks forth into the earth?

At this very moment, I'm convinced that God is desiring a great spiritual revolution concerning how we receive His Holy Word. He's desiring for His sons and daughters to become one with His Word, and for His will to be done on earth as it is in Heaven! His heart beats and desires for each and every one of us to become aligned with Him through His Word because that's how He moves and releases Himself to us, within us, and through us! It's how God determined to for His Church to resist and defeat the forces of evil, and cause Jesus to fill all things (see Eph. 6:17; Luke 4:1–13; Eph. 4:10)!

You can personally encounter God through His Word in ways you've maybe never imagined. He wants you to touch Him through the pages of the Bible and experience Him as He truly is, and not as the "World" has portrayed Him.

> *Then Jesus said to those Jews who believed Him, "If you abide in My word, you are My disciples indeed. And you shall know the truth, and the truth shall make you free." (John 8:31–32)*

THE SPIRIT OF WISDOM AND REVELATION

> *. . . that the God of our Lord Jesus Christ, the Father of glory, may give to you the spirit of wisdom and revelation in the knowledge of Him, the eyes of your understanding being enlightened; that you may know what is the hope of His calling, what are the riches of the glory of His inheritance in the saints,* (Eph. 1:17–18)

It was the first day of school, and my grade school teacher boldly declared that nothing ever got by her. Not side conversations, not notes, nothing. I thought about her comment, and as a little boy, I didn't have much of a filter and blurted out the question, "If something got past you, how would know it?" She wasn't very happy with me to say the least, but the truth remains that we're only aware of the things we're conscious of. If something gets by us, or is located in our blind spot, we aren't able to give attention to it. We don't even think about it! This is exactly why deception is so treacherous. It happens when we aren't even aware of it.

Despite the fact that Heaven longs for us to receive the Word of God as the very revelation of God Himself, earth has an extremely difficult time recognizing the many hindrances the devil throws at us. The Bible says,

> *Now the serpent was more subtle and crafty than any living creature of the field which the Lord God had made. And he [Satan] said to the woman, Can it really be that God has said, You shall not eat from every tree of the garden?* (Gen. 3:1, AMP)

The devil operates in the shadows and blind spots of our minds and emotions. He moves with such subtly that his schemes often go unnoticed. In fact, some people go throughout their lives never becoming aware the devil was busy framing their thoughts and beliefs about God.

Satan has trained people from childhood to pick and choose what they'll receive and won't receive, and what they think is acceptable or unacceptable to expect from the Word of God. We're bombarded by advertisements, messages, political agendas, and social pressure all meant to frame our worldview. **In short, satan works to get us to see the Bible through the world's eyes rather than to see the world through the Bible's eyes.**

I meet people even in the church who easily receive certain truths in the Bible, but quickly dismiss others. For example, if you ask the average Christian if they can have victory over sin through Christ, they will respond with a confident "yes." If you ask them to come and pray to raise a man from the dead, you'll probably get a look like you're the one who needs prayer even though Jesus clearly told His disciples to it.

> *Heal the sick, cleanse the lepers, raise the dead, cast out demons. Freely you have received, freely give.* (Matt. 10:8)

Both provisions are clearly in the Bible, but we've been trained and conditioned to receive some parts and dismiss others. We've been conditioned to operate in a box never created by Jesus Christ! The great deception isn't only that we have "selective" faith, but that we think it's ok!

Of course we don't wake up in the morning and declare, "Jesus, I thank You for Your Word. I believe it's perfect and infallible so I'll choose to believe the parts that are acceptable to the world around me, but I just want to let You know that I'm not going to believe the parts that stretch my natural thinking. Amen!" The subtle evaluations of God's Word happen in much deeper places of our hearts. Whether we've been deceived about the true nature of the Bible, received the lie that it's created by mankind, or that it's filled with errors, it's time we expose all hypocrisy, and allow God to bring us into the fullness of the blessings and supernatural power He's provided to us through His Word.

I heard a wonderful minister once say, "A lie believed is a lie lived!" To distrust a person's word is to distrust the person speaking it. When we hear Jesus speak and don't trust what He says, or don't receive it as complete truth, we're revealing our distrust of Jesus Himself! This is exactly why so many people say they receive and believe God's Word, but are so filled with so much doubt. They haven't come to more deeply know they can wholeheartedly trust the One who's speaking!

We desperately need to get delivered from the virus of carnal, natural, humanistic thinking when it comes to the Word of God. We need to stop relying upon others to teach us the meaning of God's Word, and need to get on our knees asking God's Holy Spirit to guide us into all truth. (See John 16:13.) We need to fast and pray and present ourselves to God and ask for His help so He may deliver us from every subtle deception the enemy tries to deploy! We need to willingly present ourselves to God and His Word and allow Him to perform spiritual surgery in us to cut out and root out every false thing we've ever received about the Word of God. We need to allow God to administer His Word like a Holy antibiotic to kill all satanic bacteria that has infected our minds and hearts concerning the Word of God! We need a new level of commitment to read and study God's Word in a way that causes its light to shine and separate every dark thing around us! Let God shine His light, and you will receive the spirit of wisdom and revelation and the eyes of your understanding will be opened! Then you will be able to operate with the power of the Holy Spirit.

MIRACLES IN THE HANDS OF A CARPENTER

And when the Sabbath had come, He began to teach in the synagogue. And many hearing Him were astonished, saying, "Where did this Man get these things? And what wisdom is this which is given to Him, that such mighty works are performed by His hands! Is this not the carpenter, the Son of Mary, and brother of James, Joses, Judas, and Simon? And are not His sisters here with us?" So they were offended at Him. But Jesus said to them, "A prophet is not without honor except in his own country, among his own relatives, and in his own house." Now He could do no mighty work there, except that He laid His hands on a few sick people and healed them. And He marveled because of their unbelief. Then He went about the villages in a circuit, teaching. (Mark 6:2–6)

A powerful example of our great need to have our eyes opened is found in the Gospel of Mark when Jesus returned to His hometown to teach in the synagogue. He came to them not as an ordinary man working the works of a natural carpenter, but rather as the Son of God working the works of God.

When the people heard Jesus teach they were astonished. He released such unique, deep, pure, and powerful things it caused them to be in wonder concerning the depth of wisdom that came forth from Him. Not only that, but they actually saw the mighty works of God come forth from His hands! Jesus did more than simply speak the Word of God, He manifested its power right before their eyes! What a shift, what a display, what a confirmation of who Jesus really was! Jesus didn't hide the power of His identity! He released it in their midst! They saw the manifested Word, and tasted its power! God the Father wanted to make His Word known, and He wanted everyone to partake of the grace and power that flowed through His Son, Jesus.

Rather than offering the Father a response of praise and thanksgiving that He sent them His Son, the Great Deliverer, they instead responded with doubt-filled questions. Questions that were fueled by their preconceived natural ideas about Jesus. We can understand their confusion because they had years of knowing Jesus as a fairly normal carpenter, and knew Him to be part of Mary and Joseph's family. They knew Jesus according to His natural identity, but were unfamiliar with His supernatural nature. The problem was that they weren't willing to see past their old, natural experience so they could behold the new, supernatural experience unveiled right in front of them! Their conviction was so strong concerning who they "thought" Jesus was that they actually became offended at Him (see Mark 6:3).

They became offended at God, and therefore couldn't receive from Him!

Jesus explained that a prophet receives honor where they're received, and does not receive honor where they aren't received (see Mark 6:4). They were so used to believing Jesus was an ordinary man they couldn't see His extraordinary deity! We're so used to thinking the Bible was written by man and filled with errors; we can't see it for the supernatural and Heavenly revelation it is! The result was Jesus was able to do no mighty work there, except lay hands on a few sick people and heal them! The Bible says that Jesus "marveled" at their unbelief. His hometown simply rejected the true nature and identity of Jesus Christ and prevented mighty and glorious things from happening! I fully believe Jesus is marveling right now with our unbelief of His Word and consequently not able to do many might works except heal a few sick people! The principle is the same now as it was then!

The lesson to us who desire to release the miracle- power of God's Word is invaluable! How we receive Jesus and His Word directly determines the level of power that will be released from Him!

When we allow our minds to conform to preconceived beliefs and refuse to see new evidence, we hinder ourselves from growing to new levels and dimensions of faith and power. The people in Jesus' hometown were exposed to the supernatural work of the Word, but snapped back into the paradigm of natural reasoning. They became victims of what I call, the "Rubber-band Effect." It's when we get stretched into new realms of faith and power, but snap back to old ways of thinking. Many times I've seen this "Rubber-band Effect" take place in the hearts and minds of God's children. The Lord will be moving powerfully as His Word is preached and people are prayed for and being healed in the Name of Jesus. The faith of the people begins to lift to new heights and their countenance change in the midst of God's presence. Then, once they leave the service or come out from under the supernatural environment, they resort back into old ways of thinking. They were astonished at the authority, wisdom, and grace of God for a moment, but fall into old patterns of natural thinking rooted in the wisdom of the world rather than the power of God!

> *And do not be conformed to this world, but be transformed by the renewing of your mind, that you may prove what is that good and acceptable and perfect will of God.* (Rom. 12:2)

The apostle Paul taught that if we're going to prove, or bring forth, the good, acceptable, and perfect will of God, then we need to be transformed by the renewing of our minds. If we're simply exposed to truth, but fail to receive it in a lasting way, change will continue to allude us. It's absolutely imperative we receive fresh revelation from the Word about the Word and never allow ourselves to become victims of our natural thinking.

> *But the natural man does not receive the things of the Spirit of God, for they are foolishness to him; nor can he know them, because they are spiritually discerned.* (1 Cor. 2:14)

The people who rejected Jesus in their hometown chose to see Jesus from a natural perspective, and therefore couldn't partake of the great grace being released from Him. The incarnate Word of God was right there, and they didn't receive Him! The creative Word of God was right in their midst ready to do mighty works, and they hindered His hand of grace! The answer to their prayers showed up, and they couldn't receive Him—even to the point that they became offended at Him!

When we receive the Bible as a natural book and fail to receive it as the supernatural revelation of God, we wind up rejecting the power of God just like the people from Jesus' hometown! We reject the very presence and power of God that's ready to perform mighty works in our lives!

Jesus may be the most famous name known throughout the world, but His Word is still too frequently received with humanistic perspectives and rarely received by the masses as the portal to God's Heavenly realm. Make the decision today to be different and to refuse to fall prey to the "Rubber-band Effect." Allow the Spirit of Holiness to open your eyes and see Jesus and His Word just as God sees it. Refuse to ever return to old ways of thinking! Think supernaturally, gaze into Jesus' face of grace, and allow God to take you from glory to glory! Allow Jesus to take you into His miracle realm. It's a key that will transform your spiritual life and allow you to access the supernatural power of God in your life.

> *But we all, with unveiled face, beholding as in a mirror the glory of the Lord, are being transformed into the same image from glory to glory, just as by the Spirit of the Lord.* (2 Cor. 3:18)

ONE TRUTH, TWO VOICES

When I became a Christian so much changed within me immediately. I knew I was a new creation in Christ. I had repented of many things, but there were mindsets, beliefs, and some habits that seemed to cling more than others. As I grew in the Word of God, I came to understand more and more that

God was a Holy God, and that He commanded us to be holy. I understood how important it was to truly repent and fully live out who we are in Christ!

The problem was that I would periodically fall into sin in a couple of areas of my life, and every time I did, I experienced an absolute horrible level of condemnation and guilt. I would kneel down and ask God to forgive me through Jesus' sacrifice on the cross. The problem was that though I did this countless times a day, I continued to feel guilty about my sin. I thought these feelings were a sign that God had not forgiven me, and that I was somehow still stained from my sin.

This cycle grew and grew and the feelings of condemnation got so bad it was as if I walked around under a ton of weight that never got removed. I thought I had sinned too much and God's grace could no longer apply to me. I thought there was no way that Jesus could possibly have mercy on me. I was just too disobedient.

One day while again on my knees pleading with God to forgive me, before I even knew what having a "vision" was, I saw Jesus far above me with His arms crossed in front of His chest and His feet shoulder width apart. I couldn't see much detail, but the picture of Jesus carried an authoritative, but comforting appearance. It was as if mercy was coming forth from the midst of His Lordship.

As I cried and pleaded for forgiveness, I became aware of a life-changing truth—Jesus was waiting for me. I remember thinking, "How could Jesus be waiting for me? I'm waiting for Him to forgive me!" The message clearly came that Jesus was waiting for me to accept His promise of grace! It wasn't that Jesus wasn't forgiving me, but it was that I wasn't receiving His forgiveness. I didn't truly receive His Word that promised I would be forgiven!

This revelation changed everything because I realized that though I didn't think I believed in a Gospel of "works", I did! Old religious teachings, beliefs, and mindsets had not been dealt with yet by the Word of God. I read the Word of God, but I didn't receive the full testimony of the Word that says,

> *If we confess our sins, He is faithful and just to forgive us our sins and to cleanse us from all unrighteousness.* (1 John 1:9)

I held onto lies the devil fed me rather than exchanging them for the truth of God's Word! I needed to receive the Gospel of grace through faith (see Eph. 2:8–9) in a deeper, more personal way! I needed to receive Unleashing Heaven's Breath!

When God makes things clear as He did that day, no time needed to pass for me to act. Right then and there I repented from mixing Gospel truth with the religion of men. I renounced deep-seeded ideas that I was accepted by God through my works. I received God's Word that promised that I was His son, and that I was forgiven! My feelings didn't matter. God's Word was true!

From that day on, I was free and able to walk in the freedom and assurance of God's forgiveness through His Son, Jesus. I understood more than ever that it was possible to know things about the Word of God and still not receive them!

GOD'S LIFE-CHANGING SEED

> *But other seed fell on good ground and yielded a crop that sprang up, increased and produced: some thirtyfold, some sixty, and some a hundred."* (Mark 4:8)

The greatest teaching on this topic concerning the impor-tance of properly receiving God's Word is found in the parable that Jesus called the parable of all parables (see Mark 4:13). It contains the foundational key to walking in and releasing the supernatural power of God. It's the parable of the sower, also called the Parable of soils, found in the synoptic Gospels in Matthew 13:1–23, Mark 4:1–20, and Luke 8:4–15.

Jesus describes that a sower went out and sowed seed. Some fell by the wayside, and the birds came and ate the seed. Some fell on stony places, and though it sprang up fast, it had no strong roots, and when difficulty came, it quickly withered. Some fell on ground with thorns, and when the thorns grew, they choked the seed. Finally, some fell on good ground, and it yielded a crop of three different sizes: some a 100-fold, some 60-fold, and some 30-fold.

Jesus plainly taught the disciples the meaning of this parable explaining the seed the sower sowed was the Word of God (see Mark 4:14). The four types of ground represent the four types of conditions of a person's heart (see Matt. 13:19; Mark 4:15). The birds of the air eating the seed from the wayward ground represent satan coming and stealing away the Word out of the hearts who didn't understand it (see Matt. 13:19; Mark 4:15; Luke 8:12). The stony places represent the person whose heart receives the Word of God with gladness but falls away when tribulation or persecution comes because of the Word (see Matt. 13:21). The thorny ground represents the heart who hears God's Word, and the cares of this world and the deceitfulness of riches and the desire for other things enter in and choke the word, causing the Word to become unfruitful (see Matt. 13:22; 4:19; Luke 8:14). The good ground are those people who hear the Word of God and have a noble and good heart, keep it, and bear fruit with patience (see Matt. 13:23 Mark 4:20; Luke 8:15).

Considering the things Jesus said reveals why this is the parable of all parables, and though it contains a multitude of lessons, its core message unlocks God's urgent cry to receive, believe, and act upon His Word! It's an enormously powerful picture of the destiny of God's Word in a person's life! It reveals the destiny of Jesus Christ in person's life! Let's dig into it a bit deeper. . .

We know the seed is the Word of God, and the Word of God was made flesh in Jesus (see John 1:14). We also know the sower is God the Father because the Father sent His only begotten Son into the world to save us. (see John 3:16). Putting this together, the parable is about the Father sowing His Son, Jesus Christ, into the hearts of people. Finally, we know there's only one seed and four types of ground. There is only one Word of God, but four heart types with four destinies.

THE WAYWARD HEART

When anyone hears the word of the kingdom, and does not understand it, then the wicked one comes and snatches away what was sown in his heart. This is he who received seed by the wayside. (Matt. 13:19)

When the Word (Jesus) falls on wayward ground, it fell into a heart that failed to receive it with understanding. It was heard, but it wasn't discerned. The person didn't protect or allow it to get rooted more deeply, and so the devil comes and snatches away the Word. The Word never had a chance to produce anything in that person's heart because it was removed! The Gospel of Luke 8:12 says, "the devil comes and takes away the word out of their hearts, lest they should live and be saved." The person never even had the chance to come to the faith in Jesus because the Word (Jesus) was removed before any change could take place. This is a sad reality because the person actually got the opportunity to get Jesus planted within them, and they allowed it to be taken away from them!

When we hear the Word of God, we need to receive it so deeply within us that the devil can't get to it. We need to guard the Word, consider it, ponder it, journal about it, read it slowly, and meditate upon it. We must be careful not to just hear God's Word and move on. We need to give it attention in such a manner that we seek to understand, discern, and protect it!

No supernatural power will be released from the wayward ground because that which produces supernatural power, the Word of God, isn't there. The devil performed an abortion with the seed before it ever had a chance to produce. No fruit can be birthed from ground that's found without seed.

Key Lesson: It isn't enough to hear the Word. It must be planted, understood, and guarded against the schemes of the enemy to take it away.

THE SHALLOW HEART

But he who received the seed on stony places, this is he who hears the word and immediately receives it with joy; yet he has no root in himself, but endures only for a while. For when tribulation or persecution arises because of the word, immediately he stumbles. (Matt. 13:20–21)

The person who received the Word of God on stony places is someone whose heart is shallow. There are too many "hard" places in the heart because it wasn't made ready for the Word of God. It wasn't prepared. There were too many things in the person's heart blocking the Word of God from going deeper.

I've met many people who say they're seeking God, but are really runners. God's Word and the Holy Spirit convict them of truth. They feel the presence of God, and sometimes even cry in response to the beauty of God's invitation to them. Nevertheless, they refuse to respond with complete submission to God's call to allow Jesus to get planted more deeply in their hearts. It appears they've fallen in love with Jesus and have received His Word, but really only allowed the Word to be planted in a shallow manner. The Word hit obstacles in their heart and wasn't able to go deeper.

The Bible says they do seemingly well for a while, but when tribulation or persecution arises because of the word, they fall and stumble. They loved the good things the Word said and promised, but because the Word never got strongly rooted in their hearts, they lacked the strength to stand strong in the face of adversity because of the Word and they fall away. Again the fruit of the Word of God got aborted further down the path, and no supernatural power will be released from this type of heart as the Word didn't continue.

Key Lesson: It isn't enough to hear the Word of God and get it planted. It must be planted so deeply that strong roots get cultivated to be able to stand strong the face of tribulation and persecution.

THE THORNY HEART

Now he who received seed among the thorns is he who hears the word, and the cares of this world and the deceitfulness of riches choke the word, and he becomes unfruitful. (Matt. 13:22)

The person who received seed among the thorns is one of the most common and tolerated spiritual conditions in America, because it gets so close to bearing fruit. It's the picture of a person who wouldn't let the devil steal the Word and removed the stony places of the heart, but still allowed their cares of this world and its temptations to remain. Things seem wonderful in this person because it seems they've made it such a long way. This condition is much more difficult to diagnose because they appear in many ways to be spiritually healthy. In fact, this heart type is especially prevalent in our western culture where it's culturally acceptable to be harried with the cares of the world, the pursuit of money, and many other desires.

In fact, sometimes preaching and teaching from the pulpits of churches even nurtures this type of heart environment focusing on how Christians can "get" the things they've always wanted—even if those things are out of alignment with God's priorities. It's the kind of preaching that carries an undercurrent of meeting the desires of an audience living for themselves rather than cultivating a holy people desiring to live for God.

The person with a thorny heart has a divided heart. They desire the Word of God, but they also still desire the glory of the kingdoms of the world. They have not completely died to themselves yet. They have not fully counted the cost of following Jesus, which is synonymous with fully meeting the requirements of His Word. These desires which haven't been crucified with Christ hinder the proper growth of God's Word. It may sound a bit dramatic to some, but the cares of this life and the deceitfulness of riches are like a cancer that chokes the spiritually clean things in a person's heart.

Still again the Bible communicates that no fruit is birthed in this type of heart and that it leads to a horrible strangling of the Word of God.

Key Lesson: It isn't enough to hear the Word, get it planted deeply, but it also needs to grow in an environment where it competes with nothing.

THE GOOD HEART

But the ones that fell on the good ground are those who, having heard the word with a noble and good heart, keep it and bear fruit with patience. (Luke 8:15)

Finally, we come to the heart that's found to be good, and able to allow the Word of God to grow. This heart has come to understand the Word of God, and withstood tribulation and persecution and has even become singular in its desire for the things of God. The devil has been able to stop nothing in the good ground because great care was taken to allow it to fully grow.

It's an amazing revelation to come to understand that the wind, the waves, the devil and his demons, the angels in Heaven, and the whole universe bow to the Word of God, but God Almighty gives us the choice to receive or reject it! Then He gives us the choice of how deeply we'll receive and follow it! It's an amazing offer God gives to each of us. He offers to allow His Word to be received, His power to mature, and His glory to be released in signs, wonders, and miracles.

The person who has a good heart is going to experience the supernatural power of God in abundance because it's no longer them who lives, but God's Word, Jesus, who lives in them. The key of all keys is to allow Jesus Christ to grow unhindered to the point that He does the living in and through us! It is the pre-existent, spoken, written, incarnate, and manifested Word that creates and frames all things! It's by faith the good ground understands the worlds were created by the Word of God and that things that are seen were not made of things that are visible.

> *By faith we understand that the worlds were framed by the word of God, so that the things which are seen were not made of things which are visible.* (Heb. 11:3)

The inner, unseen beauty and power of God's Word planted in the heart of a person, manifests glorious fruit on the outside. Some produce 30 fold, some 60 fold, and some 100 fold.

The good ground continued in the Word of God with both diligence and patience. The good heart developed an intimate relationship with the Word through study, meditation, and application. The person with the good heart not only heard the Word, but also obeyed the Word (see James 1:25) and allowed the Word to produce what only the Word could produce! It enabled that person to live with wisdom and power in such a way that manifested the Kingdom of God through its bearing of fruit. The heart and the Word of God worked together in perfect harmony and birthed great glory for God.

THE SEED OF LIFE

> *"Now the parable is this: The seed is the word of God.* (Luke 8:11)

It's so important to understand that when we look at successful Christians, we often think they are the ones producing the fruit. We think somehow they are the keys to the success. The Bible paints quite a different picture and reveals the ground does nothing but provide the environment for the seed to grow. It's the seed that contains the DNA for the fruit, not the ground.

For example, when we think about the Word of God planted in a human being like a seed being planted in the ground, it helps us understand the simplicity and power of the lesson God is teaching us concerning how to release the power of His Word.

For example, think about the seed of an oak tree. It looks fairly unimpressive and really doesn't hold much appeal to the average person. In fact, most would look at an acorn and pass by it as something unworthy of a person's attention. In fact, some may even question the purpose of an acorn. However, those with understanding know the complexity, strength, and usefulness of an oak tree is somehow packed into that small seed! They see an oak tree that will be a home to many birds, restful shade for generations, and provide wood for furniture, heat, and shelter. It may be easy to throw around an acorn, but no one can pluck an oak tree out of the ground! The strength of the seed had the opportunity to grow and mature in the ground, and its true form was eventually able to be witnessed!.

Though the inherent power of God's Word is in no way dependent on the actions of mankind, God grants the invitation for His divine power to manifest in our hearts and minds even to the point in which the apostle Paul reveals we become God's tabernacle, or temple. (See 1 Corinthians 6:19.)

The seed of God is His Word, and those who have a clear revelation of it don't just see it in its seminal, or seed form, they see by faith in its matured, or manifested form! In other words, they don't see the Bible as just an old book. They see it as the very revelation of God Himself, and the vehicle by which His miraculous power is received and released!

THE TREE OF LIFE

The thief does not come except to steal, and to kill, and to destroy. I have come that they may have life, and that they may have it more abundantly. (John 10:10)

In Genesis, the first book of the Bible, God revealed there was a tree of life in the Garden of Eden (see Gen. 2:9) that mankind was able to eat, that is, until they fell into sin. (See Genesis 3:24.) In the book of Revelation, the last book of the Bible, God revealed there is a tree of life found in the midst of the Paradise of God (see Rev. 2:7). The tree of life symbolizes God's life, and points to the person of Jesus Christ being the incarnation and manifestation of God-level, eternal life (see Gen. 3:22)!

When we plant a lemon seed, we expect a lemon tree to grow, which produces more lemons. When we produce a peach tree, we expect a peach tree to grow, which will produce more peaches. What happens when we plant the Jesus "seed," the Word of God in a person's heart? What should we expect? We should expect the manifestation of God-level life to grow within us! We should expect, in a sense, a "Jesus tree," the tree of life, to mature within us! In the Gospel of John 5:24 (NKJV), Jesus says,

> *"Most assuredly, I say to you, he who hears My word and believes in Him who sent Me has everlasting life, and shall not come into judgment, but has passed from death into life.*

The word used for life is "zoe" (Strong's Greek #2222), referring to the supernatural life of God! In John 10:10 (NKJV) Jesus says,

> *The thief does not come except to steal, and to kill, and to destroy. I have come that they may have life, and that they may have it more abundantly.*

149

The word used for life here is "zoe" (Strong's Greek #2222), referring to the same supernatural life of God! In Revelation 2:7 (NKJV), it says,

> *"He who has an ear, let him hear what the Spirit says to the churches. To him who overcomes I will give to eat from the tree of life, which is in the midst of the Paradise of God.'"*

Again, the same word "zoe" (Strong's Greek #2222) is used to describe the tree of life!

In other words, when we receive the Word of God, we receive the *seed* to the tree of life. When our heart is found to be good ground, the seed of the Word grows and matures into the tree of life! In other words, Jesus gets formed within us! Both His Person and His work become manifest through our lives. Moreover, the supernatural nature and power of the Son of God gets released like a mighty river springing forth into signs, wonders, miracles, creating complete life-transformation!

CHAPTER SUMMARY POINTS

1. The devil works violently to disconnect us from God's Word, and does all he can to place obstacles between us and Unleashing Heaven's Breath, which is the same as placing obstacles between us and God Himself! Consequently, we must be aware of the devil's schemes, and shut them down at every attempt.

2. The first and most foundational key of releasing the supernatural power of God's Word is to simply receive, believe, and act upon it. Thus, at the epicenter of the devil's strategy to prevent the supernatural power of God's Word from being

released in our lives is to try to get the Word of God from ever being received, believed, and acted upon.

3. The very first temptation recorded in the Bible recounts the devil's plot to separate mankind from God by creating enmity with God's Word.

4. It's taken generations to happen in America, but the devil has made significant inroads in our society to question, doubt, and even hold a disdain for the things of the Word of God. Though most people say they honor or believe the Word of God, the reality is that most only offer God lip service, and their hearts are far from Him.

5. No matter how much grace, how much blessing, and how much revelation God desires to impart to us, it will all be hindered if we don't receive it properly. Even our very salvation depends on how we receive the Word of God!

6. God is actively seeking those who will partner with His work upon the earth, and He's given His Word as His plumb line by which all partnering with God should occur. When our beliefs about the Bible become aligned with Heaven, the abundant grace and power of God is released! Not like a weak river, but like an exploding geyser of glory that consumes everything around it!

7. Satan works to get us to see the Bible through the world's eyes rather than to see the world through the Bible's eyes.

8. We desperately need to get delivered from the virus of carnal, natural, humanistic thinking when it comes to the Word of God. We need to stop relying upon others to teach us the meaning of God's Word, and need to get on our knees asking God's Holy Spirit to guide us into all truth. (See John 16:13.)

9. How we receive Jesus and His Word directly determines the level of power that will be released from Him! When we allow our minds to conform to preconceived beliefs, and refuse to see new evidence, we hinder ourselves from growing to new levels and dimensions of faith and power.

10. The parable of the sower teaches the importance of properly receiving and nurturing the Word of God in our lives. It teaches the condition of the heart will determine whether or not we bear fruit and release the testimony of Jesus Christ in our lives.

QUESTIONS FOR REFLECTION

1. Think deeply about how you think you've received the Word of God in your life. In what ways have you fully received it? In what ways has the enemy hindered you?

2. In what ways have your views of God's Word been aligned with Heaven? In what ways have your views been aligned with the world?

3. Review the descriptions of the four types of hearts that receive the Word of God. In what ways has your heart been wayward, rocky, thorny, or good? What practical things can you begin to do to ensure the Word of God produces 100 fold in your heart?

PRAYER

Father, I thank you for Your Word, and want to receive it exactly as it is! I renounce every lie the devil has tried to get me to agree with, and I declare I will receive, believe, and act upon Your Word in a way that's aligned with Heaven! Cause me to see Your Word with fresh, new, revelatory eyes. Show me any wayward, rocky, or thorny parts of my heart and help my heart to be good ground that receives and nurtures Your Word in a way that will produce fruit 100 fold in my life! I ask this in the Name of Jesus Christ for the glory of God! Amen!

ENDNOTES

[1] 27 Good Bible Sales Statistics-Brandon Gaille, March 5, 2015-Accessed April 29, 2016, http://brandongaille.com/27-good-bible-sales-statistics/

[2] *The Bible in America* (Ventura, CA: Barna Research Group, 2014).

Part III

THE
SUPERNATURAL
LIFE

Chapter 9

PURSUING POWER

SUPERNATURAL FOOD

*Then Jesus said to them, "Most assuredly, I say to you,
unless you eat the flesh of the Son of Man and drink
His blood, you have no life in you. Whoever eats My
flesh and drinks My blood has eternal life, and I will
raise him up at the last day. For My flesh is food indeed, and My blood is drink indeed.* (John 6:53–55)

There's an amazing phenomenon that dates back thousands
of years, and it's a source of enjoyment for tens of millions. Many
unintentionally find themselves doing it, while others go to great
lengths to participate. It can be enjoyed by young and old, it's
free, and you've probably done it many times! What is it? It's
the art of "window shopping," and the *Cambridge Dictionary*
defines it as "the activity of spending time looking at the goods
on sale in shop windows without intending to buy any of them."

Without question, too many people hear, read, and study the
Word of God like people window shop. We go to church to hear

the promises of God, study the books of the Bible, and read about the great things God has done, but rarely with a clear, focused, passionate intention of going into the "store" and owning what we see! In fact, many have come from Christian traditions that have taught that many of the supernatural promises of God aren't even meant to be experienced today! Thus, not only are people not expecting the supernatural, they also think they can't have it even if they want it!

Thank God that as a child of the most High God, you don't need to window shop the promises of God! You can experience them! You can have them! The Lord has revealed His covenants through His Word so we can not only see them, but also enjoy them! In fact, the glory of the Gospel of Jesus Christ is that the blessings and promises of God don't even need to be purchased by us. They were already purchased by God through the blood of His Son, Jesus Christ!

When God sent His Word to the earth, He desired for it to revolutionize everything in our lives. He purposed it to save us from the law of sin and death, to cause His will to be done on earth as it is in Heaven, and to be received so deeply into our lives we would become one with it! He meant to heal our bodies, deliver our minds, and make us vessels of His living glory who would go in His stead on the earth until His second coming. He purposed us to receive His Word so we can be ministers of it and bring life to the spiritually lost.

It was never meant to only be studied and analyzed, but it was meant to be spiritual food and drink. Jesus taught us in the Gospel of John that His flesh was food and His blood was drink. He said we receive eternal life when we both eat His flesh and drink His blood. Jesus was not speaking about literal consumption, but was speaking about receiving Him and His work by faith. In other words, God didn't send Jesus to merely be seen. He sent Him to be partaken of! He sent Him to be fully received so what was in His Son would manifest in those who had faith in Him. There's a big difference between merely seeing something and partaking of something. There's a big difference between being satisfied with the mere sight of something and actually owning it. Hungry people are never satisfied by seeing or even smelling the wonderful food being prepared in the kitchen. They want more. They want to eat the meal because that's the only thing that will satisfy their need.When you become born again, a hunger for God's Word is planted within you. It's a supernatural desire that God places in each one of His children because He wants them to receive all that He's provided for them. You can read the promises of God and allow the Holy Spirit to cause faith and expectation to well up within you. Your spirit should leap within you when you read about the miracle power of God! You should jump up in your seat and boldly declare, "God, I want that in my life! I want that in my body! I want that in my family! I want that in my children! I want that in my finances! I want that in my church! I want that for my eternity!" Church attenders should sit on the edge of their seats expectantly waiting to hear what great things their Heavenly Father can't wait to give them because of His great love!

Oh how our Father desires for us to desire His best! He wants us to see what He's provided and to declare, "That's for me!" "That's mine!" My Savior purchased that for me! He wants us to hunger and thirst after righteous so He can fill us (see Matt. 5:6)! You may not have known it, but God has prepared a seat for you at a table in the presence of your enemies, and your cup, right now, is overflowing!

It's simply time we move from passivity to activity as it relates to the promises of God! God wants us to move toward Him and His Word with uncompromising passion. He longs to hear us say what He heard Jacob say many years ago,

> *. . . But he said, "I will not let You go unless You bless me!"* (Gen. 32:26)

ROOF BUSTERS

> *And when they could not come near Him because of the crowd, they uncovered the roof where He was. So when they had broken through, they let down the bed on which the paralytic was lying.* (Mark 2:4)

There are three essential testimonies in life: the testimony of circumstance, the testimony of the devil, and the testimony of God's Word. The testimony of our circumstance speaks about the things that currently are. It's the current state of things and all the facts that go along with them. The testimony of the devil is the lies he speaks (see John 8:44) with the purpose of killing, stealing, and destroying. (See John 10:10.) The testimony of God's Word is the testimony of the spirit of prophecy (see Rev. 19:10) declaring the wonderful works of God for us through Jesus.

Each of us at any given time is under the primary influence of one of these testimonies. When we become too fixated on the facts of negative circumstances, we can become limited by short-sightedness and overwhelmed by situations that seem unchangeable and hopeless. When we listen to the lies of the devil, we become deceived, discouraged, and defeated. When we listen to the Word of God, we think and see like God and are filled with His faith and power to change our circumstances.

What we think and how we act reveals the testimony we've truly received.

Jesus came to the city of Capernaum and entered a man's house to preach the Word. News about it got out and spread, and the house became so filled with people that no one could fit through the door. A group of five men arrived: one paralytic and four men who carried him. When they discovered there was no room for them to enter, they came up with a radical plan. They decided they would bust through the roof to get to Jesus! Their faith was so great, their desire so strong, their determination so resolute that they would let nothing keep them from Jesus and His Word. This group of five people didn't come to window shop. They couldn't be satisfied with merely looking at the promise of God from a distance! They needed to come face to face with God's provision! They came ready to receive, and the roof was no longer an obstacle to them, it was an entrance!

I've thought about this occurrence a lot, and can't help but wonder what it was like to be there watching the expression on Jesus' face. Imagine a packed house filled with people and Jesus in the midst. Suddenly, the sound of men climbing the house is heard. Then comes the sound of the men breaking through the roof, causing pieces of debris to fall upon everyone. They keep working on the hole to get it big enough to lower the paralytic and his bed so he can get to Jesus. We don't hear that Jesus stopped the men. We don't hear Jesus reprimanding the men about interrupting His message, or about destroying the owner's property. We only learn that Jesus saw their faith and forgave the man of of his sins and healed him of his paralysis!

The great lesson here is that these men weren't passive to get to Jesus or His Word. They were hungry believers who became "roof busters" because they believed the Word enough to pursue it with a passion. They pressed through obstacles very much like the woman with the flow of blood until they could get to Jesus! The result was the releasing of a supernatural miracle! They couldn't just spectate the Word of God—they needed to "get" the Word of God at all costs.

This is the attitude God desires for us today with His Word. He doesn't long for window shoppers, who gaze at him and then depart untouched and unchanged. He desires for us to become "roof busters" in the Spirit pressing into Him and His Word!

If this paralytic lived according to his present circumstances, he would've hung his head in sadness realizing he wasn't able to get to the meeting. Instead, he got four men to carry him to the meeting. If he listened to the devil's lies, he would've been overcome with discouragement figuring God's favor wasn't upon him, and that nothing would change even if he got to the meeting. Instead, he believed God, and knew the trouble of the trip would be well worth it! He expected the supernatural. That paralytic was under the influence of the grace of God to lead him to Jesus, the forgiveness of his sins, and the healing of his body.

Simply stated, "Believers who passionately pursue God's Word in faith are going to experience the supernatural power of God's Word." They won't just look at the water in the well, they'll lower the bucket to retrieve it!

Heaven has provided and equipped us with everything we need. We simply need to dig in and lay hold of what God teaches and provides in His Word. Learn to do much more than read and study the Bible; seek its truth and revelation. Do more than window shop the promises of God. Lay hold of them! They are yours in Jesus Christ!

THE PROMISED LAND

Arise, walk in the land through its length and its width,
for I give it to you." (Gen. 13:17)

One of the greatest difficulties to a Christian's faith has to do with the sometimes large gap between the things God's Word says and the things that actually happen. If a new believer reads the Bible concerning God's promises of healing and then walks into the average church in America, they may become very confused as to why there still remains so many sick. If we read God's promises concerning financial provision and see how many Christians lack the money to meet their needs, it may become puzzling. If we read God's promises concerning His peace, but then see how anxiety-filled the average Christian is, we may become perplexed. If we see God's blessed blueprint for a healthy marriage and then come to learn the divorce rate among Christians is about the same as those who don't know Christ, we may be left asking, "Why?".

These "gaps" between what is promised and what is experienced cause many people to doubt the validity of God's Word and for some, reinforce the lie that it's simply a black leather-bound book written by man. Why should people believe it's a supernatural book if they don't see supernatural things come to pass? Thus, they trust their experience rather than God's Word!

The first key in understanding these discrepancies is to understand that God's promises are *conditional*. This may shock a lot of people because many have grown up learning that they should live their lives by "letting go, and letting God." While there's a beautiful truth behind the intention of this statement, it should more accurately be said, "Holding on, and going with

God." The fundamental misunderstanding lies in understanding the difference between God's love and God's promises.

The love of God is *unconditional*. It can't be earned, and there's nothing we could do to make God love us more. He loves the sinner and the saint the same, and even died for us while we were still yet sinners! His love is completely unconditional! God's promises, however, are conditional in that they require something in order to be put into motion. For example, the Bible says in John 3:16 that the promise of salvation is conditional,

> *For God so loved the world that He gave His only be-gotten Son, that whoever believes in Him should not perish but have everlasting life.* (John 3:16)

Nothing has to be done to be the object of God's love, but there is a "whoever believes in Him" clause that enables it to be received. In other words, only those who believe in Jesus will receive everlasting life. We also see in John 1:12,

> *But as many as received Him, to them He gave the right to become children of God, to those who believe in His name:* (John 1:12)

It was not to everyone, but to those who "received Him" that He gave the right to become children of God. God's love is 100 percent unconditional, but His promises are conditional.

A powerful illustration of this is found in the Old Testament when God led the children of Israel to the southern border of Canaan, known as the promised land. (See Genesis 12:7; 13:5.) It was an exciting time for Israel. They were at the brink of inheriting the promise of God made long ago to Abraham. God told Moses to send the leaders of each of the tribes to go and spy out the land. (See Numbers 13:1–2.) God was preparing His people to both behold and occupy their inheritance. When the 12 leaders returned after 40 days, 10 leaders came back with a bad report explaining that though it did flow with milk and honey, the land was already occupied with strong people in large, fortified cities. Caleb quieted the people and said,

> . . .*"Let us go up at once and take possession, for we are well able to overcome it."* (Num. 13:30)

In response to the great and mighty faith declaration, the other leaders said,

> . . .*We are not able to go up against the people, for they are stronger than we."* (Num. 13:31)

This confession put the entire nation into a tailspin of fear and doubt, causing them not only to doubt that the promised land had been promised, but also to doubt the faithfulness and love of God! Joshua and Caleb pleaded with the people to believe that the Lord would bring them into their land of blessing, urging them to not rebel against the Lord saying,

> *Only do not rebel against the Lord, nor fear the people of the land, for they are our bread; their protection has departed from them, and the Lord is with us. Do not fear them."* (Num. 14:9)

Joshua and Caleb knew the land was promised. They knew the Lord would be found faithful and cause them to overcome every obstacle. They even said these strong people were going to be their lunch because the Lord was with them. Unfortunately, the Word of God was not good enough for the people, and they chose to rebel against His Word. The Lord asked Moses a sad but powerful question.

Then the Lord said to Moses: "How long will these people reject Me? And how long will they not believe Me, with all the signs which I have performed among them?" (Num. 14:11)

The Lord saw and heard His people's response to His Promised Word and took it personally. He didn't ask, "Why do these people reject my promise? Or "Why don't they receive My Word?" He asked why they rejected Him and did not believe Him! This is how God responds when we don't receive and act upon His promises. When we doubt the Word of God, we doubt the One who's speaking and wind up rejecting Him! The response of God's chosen people so deeply impacted God that He wanted to wipe the people out and disinherit them! Moses interceded on behalf of the nation, and God spared them. Nevertheless, God declared no one who doubted Him would ever enter into the promised land, but would die in the wilderness (see Num. 14:23). Only Joshua and Caleb, the faithful and believing, would enter in.

The wonderful truth is that God made a promise and was faithful to it. The nation of Israel refused to yield to God's Word, and weren't able to lay hold of the promise, because they failed to fulfill their responsibility to believe God. The victory was never going to come about because of the strength of their work and effort, but was going to come about because God would bring it about. They were heirs who weren't able to inherit their inheritance. The fact that two people out of approximately 3 million made it in doesn't demonstrate a lack of God's faithfulness or His Word. It demonstrates the lack of ability of the children to receive what's been promised!

Generations later, we forget these great lessons of God and fall into fear and doubt concerning who God is and how perfect and faithful His Word is. Our God is a God of faith and His promises are received by faith. Because God and His Word are one, we can say this another way: Our God is a God of faith and His Word is received by faith! All the promises of God are yes and Amen in Jesus (see 2 Cor. 1:20) and none of them are false or "no." Every Word that God speaks is true, and not one of His Words will ever fall to the ground or come back void! Every Word will accomplish that which it has been sent to accomplish, and not one Word will ever be found false.

The reality is that because we've confused God's unconditional love with God's conditional promises, we've sunk into a tailspin of fear and doubt, causing us to receive the testimony of our circumstances or the testimony of the devil and casting aside the testimony of the Word of God. Yes, it may be that 2 out of 3 million people, less than .0001 percent, "inherit the land," but it doesn't mean God's Word is unfaithful! In fact, it means the opposite. Abraham received the promises (the Word) by faith. Joshua and Caleb received the promises (the Word) by faith, and we too receive the promises (the Word) by faith.

APPREHEND AND OCCUPY

On the same day, when evening had come, He said to them, "Let us cross over to the other side." (Mark 4:35)

There may be obstacles that present themselves between us and the Word of God, but faith in God's Word will make you resolute and enable you to press through them all so you may inherit the promises. You and I aren't called to window shop the promises of God! We're called to live in them each and every day of our lives!

If Jesus says, go to the other side of the sea even when a storm arises (see Mark 4:35), then we must go to the other side and refuse to look left or right at our circumstances. If Jesus says to us to get out of the boat in the mist of wind and waves, we must obey, walk on water, and refuse to consider the wind and the waves! (See Matthew 14:29.) If we have to press through a crowd and touch a Jewish Rabbi to make contact with the Word of God like the woman with the flow of blood, then we must do it! (See Matthew 9:21.) We must develop a spiritual mind-set and heart-set that pursues God's promises no matter what! We must live like Abraham who. . .

> . . .contrary to hope, in hope believed, so that he became the father of many nations, according to what was spoken, "So shall your descendants be." And not being weak in faith, he did not consider his own body, already dead (since he was about a hundred years old), and the deadness of Sarah's womb. He did not waver at the promise of God through unbelief, but was strengthened in faith, giving glory to God, and being fully convinced that what He had promised He was also able to perform. And therefore "it was accounted to him for righteousness." Now it was not written for his sake alone that it was imputed to him, but also for us. It shall be imputed to us who believe in Him who raised up Jesus our Lord from the dead, who was delivered up because of our offenses, and was raised because of our justification. (Rom. 4:18–25)

Abraham came to a point where he no longer considered the testimony of his circumstances. He considered only God's Word to be true! Too many give up! Too many shy back! Too many cower in the face of the Amorites, Jebusites, and giants of Anak (see Num. 13:28–29)! We are not grasshoppers in the sight of our enemy; we are strong and mighty armed with a supernatural covenant and sword that causes the strongest foes to stumble and fall in front of us. (See Numbers 13:33.) We are armed and fully girded with the Word of God because we have put on Jesus, the Word of God. (See Ephesians 6:10–17.) Even the demons believe and tremble! (See James 2:19.)

You are a child of God, and heir to the amazing, eternal, unchanging promises of God—promises that He Himself has spoken. Remember that God is not a man that He should lie (See Numbers 23:19)! He is God and God, and it is impossible for Him to lie (see Heb. 6:18)! You can trust the whole Word because if you can't trust one part, how can you have confidence to trust any of it!

You are fearfully and wonderfully made to overcome all obstacles! It's time to bust through roofs and overcome all fear and doubt. Decide to be part of the "two" who make it, and not part of the three million who don't!

Make the decision to trust God and His Word and press through everything so you may apprehend and occupy what is yours! The Word has promised you healing. (See Isaiah 53:4–5; 1 Pet. 2:24.) It's yours! Submit to God, resist the devil, cast him away, and receive what is yours! (See James 4:7.) The Word has promised you peace! Submit to God, resist the devil and his lies, cast him away, and enjoy the peace of Jesus Christ! (See John 14:27.) There are over 3,000 promises of God in the Bible, and every single one of them is "yes" in Jesus Christ!

For all the promises of God in Him are Yes, and in Him Amen, to the glory of God through us. (2 Cor. 1:20)

Do want to know why the miracle power of God's Word is released in many other countries among the poor and needy? It's not because God loves them more. It's not because of some special grace. It's because they receive and pursue God's promise with a passion! They go after it with all they have because it is all they have! Some of China's church services often last 12 hours straight, Certain Africans walk for miles on end to hear the Word of God, and countless others pursue God's promises with a passion that releases the supernatural power of God! They are authentically hungry to receive all that God has for them and God meets them in their hunger! They draw near to God and He draws near to them. (See James 4:8).

It's important to note that inheriting and living in the supernatural power of God can't be done through the works of the flesh! The promises of God aren't earned by works, but are received by and through the grace of God. Miracle-producing faith releases the promises of God, but it isn't produced by striving or human willpower. It flows out of the amazing transformations that result from being made new in Christ and abiding in Jesus. It's a supernatural outflow of being made in Christ's image! Read on to discover the amazing truth about the Word of God and the true identity of your born-again nature!

THE BABY BORN HEALTHY

Therefore I say to you, whatever things you ask when you pray, believe that you receive them, and you will have them. (Mark 11:24)

You are about to read an amazing story of how God turned an impossible situation around because a married couple clung to the promise and testimony of God's Word and pressed through amazing odds. It's written by a good friend and seven-time world Frisbee freestyle champion, Erwin Velasquez.

I grew up the baby of four children, with two brothers and a sister. Following in my brother's footsteps, I played baseball, football, and wrestled from a young age all the way through college. I excelled in every sport, and was a two-time All American wrestler qualifying for the nationals every year. In my junior year of high school, my brother and I got involved in the sport of Frisbee freestyle where we traveled the world and became seven-time world Frisbee freestyle champions. We appeared on many television shows in North America, South America, Europe, Scandinavia, and Japan. Our faces were on the back of Frisbee boxes, and one year we were featured in an Academy Award–nominated short film documentary that was shown on the Oscars program. We really felt God had blessed and poured His favor upon us.

I was introduced to Jesus Christ by my mother as a young boy, and immediately accepted Him as my Lord and Savior. I read the Word, but it wasn't until my sophomore year of high school when I really fell in love with the person of Jesus Christ, and it changed my life forever. Nevertheless, I was only able to live my Christian life according to the level of knowledge I had of Gods' Word at the time.

In the summer of 2009, my faith would be tested to its core, and would force me like never before to rely solely on the power of God's Word. Though we thought our days of diapers and heating baby bottles were over, my wife and I discovered we were expecting another beautiful child. I was going to be turning fifty years old right around the time our new baby was to be born, and I knew our world would be turned upside down.

After our first ultrasound, we were told our unborn baby girl had bad markers that were of great concern, and were indicators that our child was going to be a Down syndrome baby. They additionally showed us a flat nasal bone, eco genic bowel syndrome, cysts on her brain, and other abnormalities that only reinforced the harsh reality of the circumstances. The medical professionals urged us to seriously consider aborting the baby due to our age, and personal hardship.

After hearing this devastating news, and not knowing what to do, we turned to our Pastor, Steve Hannett of Abundant Grace Christian Church, who I knew to be a trustworthy teacher of the Word of God as well as my brother and friend. We came to him with tremendous heartache consumed with feelings of fear and abandonment. I've felt God's love, have known His spiritual embrace, and experienced His blessings. How could this happen? My unborn child was being attacked, and I felt so helpless.

Pastor Steve Hannett and his wife Kate guided us through this trying time both encouraging and assuring us that God had everything under control and that He didn't abandon us. They showed us in the Bible how God could change the outcome of any circumstance. One of the first things Pastor Steve said was, "the devil is a liar, and that if we receive and believe God's Word, our baby would be healed from what they said she had, and her health would be restored 100%."

In addition to getting us books on healing to study, Pastor Steve taught us how to speak the Word of God and command the spirit of infirmity and sickness to depart it in the Name of Jesus Christ, which we did faithfully. My wife and I prayed and encouraged each other to believe that Jesus had power to heal, and was able to correct everything the enemy was trying to destroy.

There were times where our faith faltered and we picked each other up with words of encouragement and prayer. Pastor Steve and Kate told us the enemy often tries to steal the blessing of healing after you pray and received the miracle, which was exactly what happened. We needed to make a decision whether we were going to trust God or the devil's lies. We chose to believe that we in fact did receive our healing miracle and would continue in the loving grace and healing power of Jesus Christ.

During a routine visit, her Dr. turned to her and said, "I don't care how much you pray, you're not going to take Down syndrome away from this baby." And without faltering my wife said, "You don't know my God." I get goose bumps every time I share that story. Imagine what was going on in Heaven when those words came out of her mouth!

The day finally came, her water broke, and we rushed to the hospital. I found out the delivery doctor was so sure that the baby was going to have such abnormal and severe problems that she had specialists ready to whisk the baby away from us to tend to her.

While outside the delivery room I had such intense prayer with my Father in Heaven. I prayed and had expectations of God's Word to not come back void and that he would in fact heal our baby.

The moment came and before I could even pray another prayer, the doctor held our baby up and said she was a girl, and then, as if she was proclaiming it with disbelief, said, "She's beautiful, and she seems to be normal and 100% healthy. She used the words "perfect", and "beautiful"! We got God's promise!

I could hear all of the nurses down the hallway whispering and shouting! Did you hear about the baby, . . . she's beautiful, and

100% healthy, . . . and they were saying Praise God! . . .Praise God! Hallelujah! Glory to God.

When we received the sonogram pictures, we put them on our refrigerator, but I couldn't look at them because they were a reminder to me of the bad report. God later revealed to me He didn't want me to look to the left or the right of His promises, but to remain fixed upon what He said He would do. If I looked at those pictures, it would've reinforced what the world said my reality would be, but faith doesn't operate in the natural. It operates in the supernatural!

CHAPTER SUMMARY POINTS

1. When God sent His Word to the earth, He desired for it to revolutionize everything in our lives. He purposed it to save us from the law of sin and death, to cause His will to be done on earth as it is in Heaven, and to be received so deeply into our lives we would become one with it! It was never meant to only be studied and analyzed, but it was meant to be spiritual food and drink.

2. The men who broke through the roof weren't passive to get to Jesus or His Word. They were hungry believers who became "roof busters" because they believed the Word enough to pursue it with a passion. The result was the releasing of a supernatural miracle! They couldn't just spectate the Word of God—they needed to "get" the Word of God at all costs.

3. The love of God is unconditional. It can't be earned, and there's nothing we could do to make God love us more. His love is completely unconditional! God's promises, however,

are conditional in that they require something in order for them to be put into motion.

4. Make the decision to trust God and His Word and press through everything and apprehend and occupy! Lay hold of what is yours! The Word has promised you healing. (See Isaiah 53:4–5; 1 Peter 2:24.) It's yours! Submit to God, resist the devil, cast him away, and receive what is yours! (See James 4:7.) The Word has promised you peace! Submit to God, resist the devil and his lies, cast him away, and enjoy the peace of Jesus Christ! (See John 14:27.) There are over 3,000 promises of God in the Bible and every single one of them is "yes" in Jesus Christ!

QUESTIONS FOR REFLECTION

1. Have there been promises of the Word of God that you've tended to "window shop"? You've read about them, but never expected to actually receive them? What promises has this happened the most with, and how could you shift from seeing to receiving?

2. In what areas of faith-walk have you settled with less than God's best? What things does God want you to begin to pursue with passion and bust through a roof so you may walk in the full potential of His Word?

3. Think about the Joshua and Caleb who responded with faith to enter the promised land. In what ways can you be more like Joshua and Caleb?

4. Make a list of things you will decide to apprehend and occupy in your life, marriage, family, job, health, etc.

PRAYER

Father, I want my hunger for Your Word to be stronger than it has ever been. I don't just want to read it anymore, I want to receive, believe, and act upon it. Help me to fully receive all that You desire for Your Words to produce in my life. Help me to resist both the facts of my present circumstance and the lies of the devil. I want my heart, mind, and mouth to be filled with the testimony of Your Word and I don't want to look to the left or the right of it! Father, help me to remember the words You spoke to Joshua telling him to not be afraid, so I also may stand strong in Your Power and might and walk in the fullness of Your promises. Lord, I ask all these things in the mighty Name of Jesus Christ so that Your Name will be glorified upon the earth! I ask this in the Name of Jesus Christ! Amen!

*Have I not commanded you? Be strong and of good courage; do not be afraid, nor be dismayed, for the Lord your God is with you wherever you go." (*Joshua 1:9)

Chapter 10

SUPERNATURAL WINESKINS

EVERYONE'S CALL

Heal the sick, cleanse the lepers, raise the dead, cast out demons. Freely you have received, freely give. (Matt. 10:8)

Here's great news! Each and every one of us who has become a child of God by grace through faith in Jesus Christ is called to walk in the supernatural power of God! Yes, that means you too! Every believer young, old, educated, uneducated, rich, poor, famous, unknown, etc. is meant to live a life filled with the power of God! We are meant to be walking miracles both in word and deed. We're to be so unique and different that people are supposed to ask us about the hope that's within us. We're supposed to walk as pure ambassadors of Jesus Christ upon the earth to make the beautiful Gospel of Jesus Christ known to the whole world in a way that people encounter the power of God rather than the wisdom of man (see 1 Cor. 1:24)!

This, however, will not come to pass in the lives of people if they never discover who they truly have been created to be in Jesus Christ. To learn and agree with God concerning the spiritual identity of your new born-again creation is to tap into a powerhouse of supernatural activity! I've seen people immediately transform before my eyes and watch them flow in the miracle-power of God by receiving fresh revelation of their identity and position in Jesus Christ.

Understanding your supernatural identity in Christ is more than going to encourage your Christian walk, it's going to release another key to activating the miracle power of God's Word in your life.

GOD'S CREATION

Then Zacchaeus stood and said to the Lord, "Look, Lord, I give half of my goods to the poor; and if I have taken anything from anyone by false accusation, I restore fourfold." And Jesus said to him, "Today salvation has come to this house, because he also is a son of Abraham; for the Son of Man has come to seek and to save that which was lost." (Luke 19:8–10)

Jesus said something amazing concerning His mission. He said He came to "seek and to save that which was lost." In other words, Jesus was on a mission to restore things back to a certain condition; to return things back to the way God intended them to be; and to bring things back to a former state of position or being. God the Father created things to be a certain way, and His Son was sent to return them back to a state of glory! Amazingly, we were a major focus of that restoration!

The history of creation as recorded in Genesis reveals that God created all forms of life. He created plant life, fish life, bird life (see Gen. 1:20–21), animal life (see Gen. 1:24–25), and human life (see Gen. 1:26–7). Each time God created life, He revealed a new level of complexity leading up to mankind being made in His image! God said,

> *Then God said, "Let Us make man in Our image, according to Our likeness; let them have dominion over the fish of the sea, over the birds of the air, and over the cattle, over all the earth and over every creeping thing that creeps on the earth." So God created man in His own image; in the image of God He created him; male and female He created them. Then God blessed them, and God said to them, "Be fruitful and multiply; fill the earth and subdue it; have dominion over the fish of the sea, over the birds of the air, and over every living thing that moves on the earth." (Gen. 1:26–28)*

Not only was man the only form of life on earth that was made in God's image, but man was also to have dominion over all the other life forms, including the fish of the sea, the birds of the air, and the cattle, and over everything that crept on the earth. To be made in God's image means that man must be created to rule and have authority because that's what God looks like!

> *God goes further to give greater revelation on how he created mankind. The Bible says, And the Lord God formed man of the dust of the ground, and breathed into his nostrils the breath of life; and man became a living being. (Gen. 2:7)*

First, the Lord God formed mankind from the dust of the ground. This is the natural part of our creation, and in my experience, the part that most are familiar with. In fact, when teaching about this topic in various countries, I've asked people to recall from memory what God made mankind with. Almost always, people readily remember the dust because they're familiar with natural flesh. However, God did more than form us from the dust of the ground. He breathed into Adam's nostrils, the "breath of life." This phrase "breath of life" reveals the spiritual life of God! In other words, God took His breath within Himself and breathed it into Adam. The Hebrew word for spirit is *Ruach*, meaning "wind, breath, air, and spirit". Thus, Adam went from only being a physical creature to a spiritually supernatural creation! Mankind was truly created in the image of God because he was filled the very breath or Spirit of God! (See John 4:24.)

When God formed Adam's physical body, he formed a vessel. When He breathed His Spirit into him, He filled the vessel. Adam was the first tabernacle, or dwelling place, of God upon the earth. He was God's first temple filled with His glory, and the breath of His mouth! (See Genesis 1:26–28; 2:7.)

From the very beginning, God decided to make man in His own image! God determined to fill men and women with His life, the highest form of life in all creation! Adam was one with God and walked with God, and carried God's nature, characteristics, and traits. When God looked at Adam, He was able to see His own image and called it good! Amazingly, this means there was absolutely no image of what we now know as "mankind" on the earth at this time. It may sound a bit different, but if mankind was made in the image of God, they didn't have their own image. To look at them would be to look at the image of God! Thus, the only thing creation saw when he looked at mankind was the image of God! This all means that we were literally designed to live with the life and Spirit of God to fulfill God-level, God-ordained work! We were literally designed to host His life and glory!

SIN'S CREATION

And the Lord God commanded the man, saying, "Of every tree of the garden you may freely eat; but of the tree of the knowledge of good and evil you shall not eat, for in the day that you eat of it you shall surely die." (Genesis 2:16–17)

The command for Adam and Eve to not eat of the tree of the knowledge of good and evil is probably one of the most well-known verses in the Bible. We may think about pictures of Adam and Eve by a tree about to eat an apple, or maybe we think about the idea of sin entering the world and all the things that we "shouldn't" do.

Let's step away from the whole thing for a moment and really grab a hold of what God said. Adam and Eve had been created and infused with the very life of God. Though they are glorious images of God upon the earth, they are not creators and they are not at all self-sufficient. All that's good in them is God Himself. Their "image" is completely dependent on God.

In addition, they were created by God's Word and living in the creation created by God's Word. In other words, everything both in them and around them was determined and set by God's Word. They were entirely surrounded by the production of God's Word, and it was paradise! When God commanded the man to not eat of the tree of the knowledge of good and evil, it was more than a recommended idea to help them have a better life! It was not about morality or anything like that. God said that if they disobeyed Him and ate the tree they would die that very day. In other words, their life and death all hinged upon whether they would continue in God's Word. If they didn't continue in His Word they couldn't continue in God's life.

Some have wondered how Adam and Eve could've still walked upon the earth, had children, etc. if God said they were going to die once they ate of the tree. The question is easily understood when we realize God wasn't speaking about the life of their natural, physical bodies, but was speaking about the departure of His Spirit-life that He breathed into them.

When most people think of death, they think of something that ceases to exist; however, the Bible reveals that death for human beings is actually a condition or state of being. The scientific definition of cold is the absence of heat. The scientific definition of darkness is the absence of light. Thus, it's easy to understand that the definition of death is simply the absence of life!

Once Adam and Eve chose to hear and listen to the wrong voice speaking the wrong word, they fell into sin and the life of God's presence immediately departed from them. Satan's voice of temptation was designed to get Adam and Eve to receive, believe, and act upon his word, which was devoid of the life, love, power, and presence of God. When Adam and Eve listened to the word devoid of God's love and life, they came under the deadly poisonous influence of the devil and received its fruit. In other words, God's Word is a seed that contains life, and to receive this seed is to receive life. Satan's word is a seed of death, and to receive that seed is to receive the only thing it's able to produce, which is death.

When God's life departed from Adam and Eve, they no longer bore His image. They were no longer temples of His life, but became temples of that which was empty and void of Him. In short, they were filled with darkness and death. They were no longer temples, but became tombs.

The law of creation in Genesis is that "everything reproduces according to its own kind." (See Genesis 1:11,12,21,24,25;6:20;7:14.) Because Adam and Eve no longer bore the image of God upon the earth, they could no longer produce the image of God upon the earth. Therefore, when Adam and Eve had children, they weren't producing according to God's image, but were producing according to the image of fallen man. (See Genesis 5:1–3.) God reveals that this sin condition didn't just stop with Adam and his children, but continues through every generation today! The Bible even reveals that we were "children of wrath" before we received the grace of God through Jesus! (See Ephesians 2:3.)

THE GOSPEL OF LIFE

"Most assuredly, I say to you, he who hears My word and believes in Him who sent Me has everlasting life, and shall not come into judgment, but has passed from death into life. (John 5:24)

To some, Jesus Christ was a good teacher of basic wisdom and morality, and Christianity a religious, philosophical ideology that champions brotherly love and charitable works that have a positive influence on society. Frequently, the message of the cross is reduced to "repent or go to hell", and people fall into the trap of attempting to change their behavior in their own strength, while figuring out what is, and is not, morally acceptable in a fallen world that doesn't know which end is up!

This great departure from the core message of the Good News of Jesus Christ has greatly contributed to nominal Christianity, and caused many to completely miss the Person and Work of Jesus Christ. Though Christianity certainly teaches that we should turn away from sin, change our behavior, and perform works of love, these things are not the core message. They are only the things that flow out of the primary work of Jesus Christ!

When God saw the world after the Fall of Man, He saw a realm that was brought under the influence of darkness through sin. Generation after generation, mankind continued to reject God and rebel against His Word! Nevertheless, God's relentless love pursued us and sent His Son, Jesus Christ, to come save that which was lost, to solve the death problem among men, and to once again put His spiritual life into restoring us as temples of His life and Spirit!

Our eyes see people living, walking, playing, laughing, dancing, working, vacationing, eating, etc. We think things are going well if we're not in pain and when our loved ones are feeling well. If a person goes to church and reads the Bible occasionally and hasn't murdered anyone, we think they are definitely going to Heaven because they have more "good works" than bad. The problem is we have a short-sighted vision imprisoned to the natural realm. God's eyes pierce the spiritual realm, and His heart aches because He sees the true condition of things.

Proof to this is the common misperception that judgment of whether a person will spend eternity in Heaven or hell happens after they die. Though there is a judgment that happens after we die, it is not the judgement of where they will spend eternity. That judgment of where someone will spend eternity takes place here and now on the earth! Let's examine it with a verse almost every Christian has heard and can even quote, John 3:16.

For God so loved the world that He gave His only be-gotten Son, that whoever believes in Him should not perish but have everlasting life. (John 3:16)

The verse says that God so loved the world that He gave His Son, Jesus, that whoever believes in Him wouldn't die but would go to Heaven. Amen! However, the reality is that if God didn't send Jesus to save us from the death then there would be no way for them to be saved! In other words, people would already be condemned to die because of the judgement that was already upon them because of their sin.

Now let's look at a verse that many Christians have never heard and few can quote, John 3:18.

"He who believes in Him is not condemned; but he who does not believe is condemned already, because he has not believed in the name of the only begotten Son of God. (John 3:18)

This is a powerful and weighty verse that reveals that the person who believes in Jesus "is not condemned." That's the present tense. Right here, right now, if a person believes in Jesus, they are not condemned. They are saved right now! But, he who does not believe is condemned already! The judgment of that person's life isn't something that will take place later, but is something that is taking place right now! The key to understanding all of this is that we don't start out alive and then lose life and go to hell, but rather we start out with a nature bent away from God (see Gen. 5:1–3; Rom. 5:14). We start out void and empty of God. Said another way, we start out dead because of both the condition and actions of sin.

When traveling and ministering among churches, I frequently ask whether any believer in Christ has ever personally met someone who has been brought back from the dead. Most look around to see if anyone has only to find that most have never. I then have them turn to Paul's letter to the Ephesians, Chapter 2, verse 1, which reads:

And you He made alive, who were dead in trespasses and sins, (Ephesians 2:1)

Immediately people see the point. They all know someone who has been brought back from the dead! Themselves! Every believer was dead in trespasses and sins, and God sent His Son, Jesus, to make us alive! This is what the work of Jesus' resurrection is all about! He took our sin and death, paid its penalty, and overcame death on the third day in His resurrection! The Bible says that death couldn't hold Him! Oh death where is thy victory? This is the core message of the Good News of Jesus Christ! He has overcome death, and all who believe in Him can become alive in Him!

This is not simply a behavioral change! This is a literal and amazing regeneration of the human being to put back the "zoe" life of God into mankind! Jesus' coming to the earth was one enormous rescue mission from death! Yes, according to John 5:24, those who hear God's Word and believe in Him have everlasting life, won't come into judgment, and have passed from death to life!

He who has the Son has life; he who does not have the Son of God does not have life. (1 John 5:12)

FROM TOMB TO TEMPLE

Or do you not know that your body is the temple of the Holy Spirit who is in you, whom you have from God, and you are not your own? (1 Cor. 6:19)

From the first book of Genesis to the last book of Revelation, God has desired His dwelling place to be with mankind. It's a theme interwoven throughout the Scriptures that God creates a vessel, and then desires to fill it with His presence.

As mentioned, the first dwelling place of God upon the earth was Adam, whose body was meant to be a container for the Spirit of God. Then we see the Tabernacle God instructed Moses to build in the wilderness which contained the Ark of the Covenant symbolizing the presence of God with His people. God gave Moses divine instructions to build the tent, and then filled it with His Shekinah Glory. (See Exodus 25:8–9.) Next, Solomon built a more permanent temple meant to testify of the greatness of God, and God filled the temple with His presence. (See 1 Kings 8:10–12; 1 Chronicles 28:6.) That temple was destroyed because the people turned to idols, and Zerubbabel built the next temple (see Ezra 3:12; 6:15, 16) that God put His Spirit in it also. Finally, Herod's temple was built with no mention of God's glory filling that temple. Instead, Jesus made a whip of cords and drove out all the people, animals, and money changers declaring that His Father's house should not be made a house of merchandise. (See John 2:15–17.) Indeed, every earthly, natural tabernacle, or dwelling place, was only a replica or foreshadowing of God's ultimate plan to restore His dream of His people once again being His dwelling place.

The coming of Jesus Christ to the earth is the coming of the true and perfect temple of God the Father! Once again, the perfect image of God was upon the earth in the likeness of a man! When Philip asked Jesus to show them the Father, Jesus said,

> . . . *"Have I been with you so long, and yet you have not known Me, Philip? He who has seen Me has seen*

the Father; so how can you say, 'Show us the Father'?
(John 14:9)

Jesus was and is the perfect image of the Father! He is the true temple of God! In fact, after Jesus cleansed the temple in Jerusalem, He explicitly revealed that He was God's living, breathing temple! He said,

> *Jesus answered and said to them, "Destroy this temple, and in three days I will raise it up." Then the Jews said, "It has taken forty-six years to build this temple, and will You raise it up in three days?" But He was speaking of the temple of His body.* (John 2:19–21)

This means that according to the law of creation in Genesis that says everything reproduces "according to its own kind," Jesus can reproduce who He is, and He's the temple of God. Thus, the Good News of Jesus Christ is that Jesus fully assumed our spiritual condition of being a death-filled tomb in order to make us life-filled temples! He was once again going to enable mankind to be a glorious temple for the Spirit of God to dwell. During Jesus' suffering on the cross, He said,

> *Now when the sixth hour had come, there was darkness over the whole land until the ninth hour. And at the ninth hour Jesus cried out with a loud voice, saying, "Eloi, Eloi, lama sabachthani?" which is translated, "My God, My God, why have You forsaken Me?"* (Mark 15:33–34)

It was at this point that because Jesus became sin (see 2 Cor. 5:21) and became cursed (see Gal. 3:13) that God the Father could no longer dwell with Him and departed from Him!

The glorious truth is that because Jesus had never sinned, and only took our sin upon Himself to fulfill the righteousness of

God, death never had any legal right over Him. In fact, Jesus had to lay down His life because it couldn't be "taken" by the devil. The devil had no power over Him because Jesus never sinned. Death only has power when there is sin. (See 1 Cor. 15:56) The Father had to offer His Son, Jesus, as a sacrifice, the "Lamb of God," and Jesus had to "lay down" His life for us, because the devil couldn't take it! He never had any authority over Jesus!

Thus, Jesus' dead body was placed in a tomb (see Matt. 27:59–60) symbolizing the death condition and destiny of our sin, but on the third day rose again and walked out of the tomb. Jesus wasn't in the tomb because He was overcome by death. He was in the tomb because He was overcoming death! It's devastating to think about, but Jesus Christ became a death-filled tomb so we could become temples filled with His life! What a glorious moment it must have been when the Spirit and life of God the Father was breathed back into Jesus and life arose where death once reigned!

When Mary and the other women searched for Jesus at the tomb the angels said,

> . . . *Why do you seek the living among the dead? He is not here, but is risen! . . .* (Luke 24:5–6)

> *And so it is written, "The first man Adam became a living being." The last Adam became a life-giving spirit. However, the spiritual is not first, but the natural, and afterward the spiritual. The first man was of the earth, made of dust; the second Man is the Lord from heaven. As was the man of dust, so also are those who are made of dust; and as is the heavenly Man, so also are those who are heavenly. And as we have borne the image of the man of dust, we shall also bear the image of the heavenly Man.* (1 Cor. 15:45–49)

What an amazing truth! The first Adam became a living being, but Jesus, the second Adam or "last," Adam became a life-giving Spirit! The first Adam received spiritual life, and the last Adam gives spiritual life! The first Adam breathed "in" life, and the second Adam breathed Activating God's Miracle Power of life into us! As the first Adam was, so are those who are made in the image of the first Adam; nothing but a tomb of dust! However, the wonderful, awesome, and amazing truth of the Gospel is that as the Heavenly Man is, so shall we be who believe in Jesus! We are born again according to His Heavenly image! We have once again been restored to be like Jesus . . . temples of the living God and His Holy Spirit! The Bible says,

> *Or do you not know that your body is the temple of the Holy Spirit who is in you, whom you have from God, and you are not your own?* (1 Cor. 6:19)

> *And when He had said this, He breathed on them, and said to them, "Receive the Holy Spirit.* (John 20:22)

SUPERNATURAL DNA

> *having been born again, not of corruptible seed but incorruptible, through the word of God which lives and abides forever,* (1 Pet. 1:23)

To fully grasp the depth of our identity in Christ, we need to not only know that we've received Jesus's life and that we've been made temples of His Holy Spirit. We need to understand the spiritual DNA of our born-again creations.

First, we need to grasp the reality that when we are born again, we are not "improved" on. We're literally made completely new creations! The Bible says,

> *Therefore, if anyone is in Christ, he is a new creation; old things have passed away; behold, all things have become new. (2 Cor. 5:17)*

Our old nature has passed away! We are no longer who we used to be! We have become a brand new creation, and one that is not born of the natural world, but of the spiritual world! Jesus said,

> *That which is born of the flesh is flesh, and that which is born of the Spirit is spirit. Do not marvel that I said to you, 'You must be born again.' (John 3:6–7)*

Our natural bodies may have been born of flesh, but our spiritual bodies are born of Spirit! Just like Adam was first born of the dust of the earth, so we're first born of the dust of the earth. As Adam received God's breath making him spiritually alive so we receive God's breath and are made alive! We are literally born of God!

What exactly is God's breath? It's the very essence of who He is and the spiritual life within Him! It's the Word of God, Jesus Christ!

We know God's Word made everything and that includes our born-again spiritual bodies! The Bible says in 1 Peter 1:23 that we were born not of a seed that dies, but of the seed that is eternal through the Word of God! In other words, if we were to look at the genetic seed of a natural Father, we would see the characteristics of his DNA in his son. In the same way, because we have been begotten of Christ, we are begotten of His seed, the Word of God, and that which is in Him, is in us! Our born-again natures are made in Christ's Heavenly image (see 1 Cor. 15:45) because we are begotten of that which He is made of, God's Word! Our new birth is made His image! We carry the supernatural DNA of Jesus Christ!

First, God released Himself in the beginning by saying, "let there be light" (see Gen. 1:3) because He is light. Second, Jesus revealed that He is the "light of the world" and separates us from darkness, and then God's Word calls those who believe in Him the "children of light"! The Bible says,

For you were once darkness, but now you are light in the Lord. Walk as children of light (Eph. 5:8)

You are all sons of light and sons of the day. We are not of the night nor of darkness. (1 Thessalonians 5:5)

Children of God are so much more than we've appreciated or understood! We are literally born of God! The Gospel of John says,

who were born, not of blood, nor of the will of the flesh, nor of the will of man, but of God. (John 1:13)

When God sees His Word, He sees the image of His Son. When God sees His Son, He sees His Word. When God sees those begotten of the Word of God, He sees His children, and when He sees His children, He sees His Word! God once again, following the sacrifice of His Son, is able to see His image in us upon the earth and calls it good!

When we received the Word of God, we received Jesus and became saved from eternal death. We were saved from eternal death because we received eternal life because Jesus Christ is eternal life (See John 11:25) as God's Word is eternal!

having been born again, not of corruptible seed but incorruptible, through the word of God which lives and abides forever, because "All flesh is as grass, And all the glory of man as the flower of the grass. The grass withers, And its flower falls away, But the word of the Lord endures forever." Now this is the word which by the gospel was preached to you. (1 Pet. 1:23–25)

Listen to how the New Testament describes someone who is saved! They are someone who received the Word of God!

Now when the apostles who were at Jerusalem heard that Samaria had received the word of God, they sent Peter and John to them, (Acts 8:14)

Now the apostles and brethren who were in Judea heard that the Gentiles had also received the word of God. (Acts 11:1)

These were more fair-minded than those in Thessalonica, in that they received the word with all readiness, and searched the Scriptures daily to find out whether these things were so. (Acts 17:11)

And you became followers of us and of the Lord, having received the word in much affliction, with joy of the Holy Spirit, (1 Thessalonians 1:6)

As the Word of God is supernatural, you who are begotten of the Word are every bit as much supernatural. We are heirs and joint-heirs of Christ (see Rom. 8:17)! Our old natures have been crucified, and it should no longer be us who live, but Jesus Christ who lives within us! (See Galatians 2:20.) When Jesus became transfigured on the Mount in Matthew 17, it was as if he peeled back His flesh to reveal the glorious supernatural nature we were going to partake of through Him! When a person embraces that they are more than natural flesh and they are temples of the living, breathing, moving, miracle-working Word within them, they will live differently! They can begin to declare that they are more than meets the eye! That they have been fearfully and wonderfully been made by God's Word!

When the devil sees a believer in Jesus Christ, he sees more than just their natural nature! He sees the glory as of the only begotten of the Father living inside you! He trembles at the very thought that God's Word has begotten us! As the apostle Paul proclaimed,

> *that you put off, concerning your former conduct, the old man which grows corrupt according to the deceitful lusts, and be renewed in the spirit of your mind, and that you put on the new man which was created according to God, in true righteousness and holiness.* (Eph. 4:22–24)

It's time that we as believers see ourselves as God sees us and not as the world sees us! It's time we no longer focus on living in, and for the flesh, but live in, and for God according to who we really are in Christ. When we lift weights at the gym to build muscle, we're taking care of our natural bodies and packing on some more dust. When we exercise to lose weight, we're taking care of our natural bodies to shed a little dust. When we get haircuts and put make up on, we're making our dust look good! These things may all be fine, but we need to primarily focus on developing spiritual strength and live in the spirit by edifying and growing in the Word of God!

> *For bodily exercise profits a little, but godliness is profitable for all things, having promise of the life that now is and of that which is to come.* (1 Tim. 4:8)

Make a new commitment today to put off your old man and live according to the new man created according to God! You are supernatural and more than capable to work miracles in the Name of Jesus Christ! You can heal the sick, cleanse the lepers, and raise the dead! Your born-again nature is a supernatural wineskin, and it's filled with the Word of God! Go for it!

FROM CRIMINAL TO CHRISTIAN

The following story is written by someone whose name we're unable to publish due to his past criminal activity. He's someone who went from being a drug dealer in the streets to serving as a Deacon in his church. He's someone who received God's Word and became a new creation. Here's his story . . .

1979, the birth of a new decade was coming. I thought I was being cool, but what did I know? Just hanging out on the street corner, I never saw what was coming. I really do wish my memory of the eighty's was better so I could give a more detailed account, but to this day that whole decade is a blur. Looking back, I honestly don't want to remember.

In 1980, I was fourteen years old and a Freshman in high school. These should have been the best years of my life. They weren't and they weren't for many people that I knew. This was a time of serious drug use, drug dealing, stealing, fighting, sex abuse, suicide attempts, and only destruction. I can say this was the lowest point I ever hope to see in life.

I hated everyone and everything. Life was just waiting for the next high. I would get high on my way to school, on the days I went to school, then get higher when I was there. I would stop in on occasion to beat someone up, or see a girlfriend. I was so disruptive;

I was bounced out of every class. Freshman year. I had eight study hall classes, no classes. In fact, some study hall teachers wouldn't accept me, so I sat in the principal's office. I was uncontrollable, and I thought it was cool.

By 1982, I was thrown out of school and started my first part-time job. I liked to work even for minimum wage ($3.35 an hour). This is the point I realized drugs were expensive. So, I went into "business" for myself. After all, why should I pay to get high when I could get high and make money too. I was a very popular dealer; I always had something in stock. Soon things escalated from selling dime bags of weed to hard drugs. Pills were very popular at the time, with pills came sex, again I was very popular, always available. I had no problem dealing with older criminals; I was being groomed for prison. None of my relationships with women lasted but a few months at most; women were disposable like trash. There was always another one around the corner.

Let's fast forward to 1983; I got my driver's license. I was happy and started as an apprentice in a garage. I was actually good at mechanics when I showed up. I liked the work; money was better too.

I thought this was the high point of my life, I really did. About this time, I found out that I could make even better money stealing cars and motorcycles, so I fell in with that crowd. With improved funding, I found a new hobby, cocaine and speed; sex was even better on coke; again, I was very popular. This is where I remained until about 1993; I was a functioning drug addict; I always worked. I had my own apartment by 1990 and liked a steady paycheck. I remember my neighbors laughing when I was stealing cable television.

My dearest friend called me in early 1994, April I think. She was the only one who seemed to care. Even my own mom described me as mean, can't blame her. I was invited to a barbeque; I hadn't seen her for maybe three years; she was married now. I decided to go; I was thinking party time. It turned out to be a real drag; I couldn't wait to leave. It was nice to see my friend was well anyway. We were saying goodbye in her driveway when a hot blond pulled up in a ratty Chevy Caprice. I thought this might turn this party around. We walked over to say hello, and I noticed a Bible on the seat next to her. Didn't mean anything to me, she was hot. They convinced me to stay and have coffee before the drive home, I agreed. The conversation quickly turned to some guy named Jesus. They told me many strange things, He loves me, He died for me, He wants to save me. They spoke to me for about two hours, Boom, no effect! I thought I had escaped when I left for home.

The drive home was about an hour, but it seemed like two. Everything they said to me kept echoing in my head, someone loves me? Someone died for me? I pulled into my parking space and couldn't shut the car off. Who is this Jesus guy? I drove to the bookstore and bought a Bible. When finally home, I started reading, I couldn't find this Jesus. The name isn't mentioned in Genesis, after a while I gave up. A week later, my friend called to say thank you for going to the barbeque. I asked her where is Jesus in the Bible, total silence! She started laughing and praising God, then she told me what to read. I kept trying to read but couldn't understand; I was still high. She invited me to church. Within another few months, I was putting Gospel tracts in with my "products." Needless to say, my customers were not happy. Suddenly people stopped calling; business was gone. I was still getting high, but no one wanted my business. By September, I was baptized. I thought things were good; even my boss said I turned into the model employee, but . . .

One day shortly thereafter, I had a really strange day, I was filled with dread. I could think of nothing but death and dying; I wanted to die. I kept thinking if Jesus wants me, I will go see Him that night. When I got home from work, I had my last meal. I went into my bedroom and closed the door, I will long remember the feel of cold steel in my hand, a Colt .45 would take my head clean off, I wanted to pray first. I was crying and whimpering like a wounded puppy. Wiping the tears from my face on the carpet, I remember asking Jesus to take away these horrible feelings. As long as I live, I will swear I felt a hand on my back. I didn't hear anything, but I was touched by the King! My dread instantly turned to joy. I was making up a song called God is Great, I should have written that down. That was the very moment of Salvation. Blessed is my Savior!

It has been a long road. Sometimes easy, sometimes not so easy. I stand on the promise Jesus gives all of us. I will never leave you nor forsake you (see Heb. 13:5). The road of salvation is a long one but after all these years remembering where I was, and seeing where I am, all praise goes to the God who saves. I cannot look at myself objectively. I can only describe my transformation by quoting our beloved Paul.

Now the works of the flesh are evident, which are adultery, fornication, uncleanness, lewdness, idolatry, sorcery, hatred, contentions, jealousies, outbursts of wrath, selfish ambitions, dissensions, heresies, envy, murders, drunkenness, revelries, and the like . . . Those who practice such things will not inherit the Kingdom of God (see Gal. 5:19–21). This was my life before meeting Jesus. Never a hope. But the fruit of the Spirit is love, joy, peace, long suffering, kindness, goodness, faithfulness, gentleness, self-control (see Gal. 5:22–23). This is my life after meeting Jesus. Yes tribulations come, and no,

I have not been perfect. However, there is no comparison between these two lives I've led. I praise God for allowing me to see both sides of life. I have a new agenda in life. To live pleasing to my Lord who would not let me go. To live by the principles He set for me in His Bible. This is life. My life began and ended at a little hill called Calvary outside the gates of Jerusalem 2000 years ago where my Savior died that I might live. Amen.

CHAPTER SUMMARY POINTS

1. Each and every one of us who has become a child of God by grace through faith in Jesus Christ is called to walk in the miracle power of God!

2. Jesus said something amazing concerning His mission. He said He came to "seek and to save that which was lost." Amazingly, we were a major focus of that restoration!

3. From the very beginning, God decided to make man in His own image! God determined to fill men and women with His life, the highest form of life in all creation! When God looked at Adam, He was able to see His own image and called it good!

4. Once Adam and Eve chose to hear and listen to the wrong voice speaking the wrong word, they fell into sin and the life of God's presence immediately departed from them. Satan's voice of temptation was designed to get Adam and Eve to receive, believe, and act upon his word, which was devoid of the life, love, power, and presence of God. When God's life departed from Adam and Eve, they no longer bore His image. They were no longer temples of His life, but became empty tombs void of God. In short, they were filled with darkness and death.

5. Every believer was dead in trespasses and sins, and God sent His Son, Jesus, to make us alive! This is what the work of Jesus' resurrection was all about! He took our sin and death, paid its penalty, and overcame death on the third day in His resurrection! This is a literal and amazing regeneration of the human being to restore the "zoe" life of God in mankind!

6. The first Adam received the breath of life, and the second Adam gave the breath of life to us! After being born again, we now bear His Heavenly image! We have once again been restored to be like Jesus . . . temples of the living God and His Holy Spirit!

7. We have been begotten of Christ, we are begotten of His seed, the Word of God, and that which is in Him, is in us! Our born-again natures are in Christ's Heavenly image (see 1 Cor. 15:45) because we are made of that which He is made of, God's Word! We are restored in His image!

QUESTIONS FOR REFLECTION

1. Do you truly believe you've been called to live and operate in the supernatural power of God? Why, or Why not?

2. What does it mean that God's life, through Jesus Christ, has been imparted to me? What does it mean that I've been made alive in Jesus?

3. Describe the kind of intimacy your Heavenly Father desires with you now that you know He desires for you to be His dwelling place.

4. How would your life and/or ministry change if you fully lived with a clear understanding of your identity in Christ? Your family? Your church?

PRAYER

Father, I receive my call to operate in the supernatural power of God! I refuse to see myself the way others see me and desire to see myself only the way You see me! Establish me in my supernatural identity as Your son/daughter! I recognize that I am alive in You and that my born-again creation is made in Your image and that I'm filled with Your Word and Your Holy Spirit! Strengthen me to never bring anything from the world into this temple, but to only be filled and consumed with Your Word and Spirit! Establish me in Your Word so Your Word may produce every good thing so You may be glorified! I ask this in the Name of Jesus Christ! Amen!

Chapter 11

Undefeated Living

Expecting Greatness

By the word of the Lord the heavens were made, And all the host of them by the breath of His mouth. He gathers the waters of the sea together as a heap; He lays up the deep in storehouses. Let all the earth fear the Lord; Let all the inhabitants of the world stand in awe of Him. For He spoke, and it was done; He commanded, and it stood fast. (Ps. 33:6–9)

Now that we've learned so much about the true identity of God's Word, how to encounter it with power, and the true nature of our born-again creations, we can better understand the amazing potential of releasing it in our lives and the lives of others.

To live by the Word of God is to live by that which made the Heavens and all who dwell in them. It's the highest level of living, and there's no greater authority in all creation other than God's Holy Word! All things are under its authority, and we should come into the presence of God with awe that "He spoke, and it was done; He commanded, and it stood fast." (See Psalm 33:9)

All that God has spoken in His Word are true and shall be accomplished. Not one Word of God will ever be found untrustworthy, and not one Word of God will ever return to Him void. God says,

"For as the rain comes down, and the snow from heaven, And do not return there, But water the earth, And make it bring forth and bud, That it may give seed to the sower And bread to the eater, So shall My word be that goes forth from My mouth; It shall not return to Me void, But it shall accomplish what I please, And it shall prosper in the thing for which I sent it.
(Isa. 55:10–11)

God's Word has accomplished, and will accomplish, everything He's purposed it for, and every believer yoked to Jesus should be expectant for Him to fulfill it in their lives! Heaven is excited when a believer shifts from following the wisdom of the world to following the supernatural Word of God. Heavenly hosts know the glory of God is about to break out in that person's life. They know the devil will be shut down and works of God will prosper! Even angels are excited because they also serve and follow God's Word as the Psalms teach us . . .

Bless the Lord, you His angels, Who excel in strength, who do His word, Heeding the voice of His word.
(Ps. 103:20)

MAKING THE SHIFT

Trust in the Lord with all your heart, And lean not on your own understanding; In all your ways acknowledge Him, And He shall direct your paths. (Prov. 3:5–6)

No matter how much we may know about the Word of God or how much we may appreciate its value, its true purpose in our lives will never be realized until we learn to live in it and by it the way God designed. Thus, it's essential we learn how to live with the Word of God in a way that's going to release its supernatural power. This will prove to produce the miracles, signs, and wonders only the Word of God is capable of producing! This is the way to victorious living. The Word has never been defeated, and to live by it is to live undefeated.

We should realize, however, that to truly live according to the principles, teachings, and instructions of the Word of God presents a significant shift from how we usually live. The general concepts of living by God's Word are simple, but nevertheless fairly radical in our culture as they call for us to live by faith and not by sight. (See 2 Cor. 5:7.) It challenges us to trust the Lord with all our hearts, and not to lean on our own understanding (see Prov. 3:5–6).Some may try to approach the decision to live by God's Word through sheer willpower, and that's a recipe for disaster. If we were able to simply live by God's Word through human effort, Jesus would never have had to send the Holy Spirit to empower us for spiritual living. Living by the Word of God must be done by the empowerment of God from the beginning to the end.

We have to appreciate that most of us have lived outside the Word of God for many years before coming to Christ, and some have even continued outside the Word of God while being saved! The sad truth is many people have gotten saved, but have never had the opportunity to get discipled or mentored by experienced and mature believers. This has contributed to making people used to "not" living by the Word of God.

When Adam and Eve were first created, they were able to live by the Word of God. When the life and Spirit of God departed from them, they no longer could live by the Spirit, but lived in the realm of soul and body. To be led by the body is to be led by its needs and desires—a dangerous proposition to say the least. To be led by the soul is to be led by the needs and desires of our mind, will, and emotions. The vast majority of our lives are lived in the context of these two realms. In fact, we're so used to living in the realms of body and soul that living according to the Spirit can be a scary proposition. As we saw in Chapter 4, the devil tempted Jesus in these realms and Jesus responded by telling him that

> . . . 'Man shall not live by bread alone, but by every word that proceeds from the mouth of God.'" (Matt. 4:4)

When we fail to live by the Word of God, we suffer in the work of our own hands. As soon as Adam and Eve fell, they knew they were naked and felt shame. In response to their need, they turned to the work of their own hands and made coverings from fig leaves. We must be careful that as Christians, we live by the finished work of Christ and not by the works of our flesh. This is why Jesus told us that we needed to follow Him! He boldly said,

> Then Jesus spoke to them again, saying, "I am the light of the world. He who follows Me shall not walk in darkness, but have the light of life." (John 8:12)

It's a new day, and God is ready to have you not just read His Word, not just meditate on His Word, but follow His Word! It may take time to come to live more fully by the Word of God, but all who've made the shift taste the glory of God and never want to go back to being led by body and soul. They have tasted the goodness, strength, and power of God's Word and come to cherish it as much as the air they breathe.

HEAVEN'S EXPECTATION

"Most assuredly, I say to you, he who believes in Me, the works that I do he will do also; and greater works than these he will do, because I go to My Father. And whatever you ask in My name, that I will do, that the Father may be glorified in the Son. If you ask anything in My name, I will do it. (John 14:12–14)

One of the simplest but profound things to learn is that Heaven actually expects us to follow God's Word. It may seem too simple to even mention, but I nevertheless know it's necessary. We are culturally accustomed for it to be acceptable to receive only some of what God says rather than everything He says. For example, we receive that we shouldn't lie, steal, or commit adultery, but do we really accept that we should financially give as we are able? Do we keep the Sabbath holy? Do we really pray unceasingly? Do we really endeavor to live by every Word that proceeds from the mouth of God?

As we saw earlier, Peter asked Jesus to command him to come out and walk on the water. Peter wasn't just asking God to change locations; he was seeking to be with Jesus and experience His power. Though it was still dark, though there were no life preservers, though there were no ropes attached to Peter, and though they were in the middle of a storm, Jesus never told Peter to stay in the boat. He never told him that he was asking for too much or that it wasn't a human being's place or that He really never meant for Peter to get out of the boat when He said, "Come." Not at all. Jesus welcomed Peter to walk on top of the water. **Jesus expected Peter to trust and walk upon His Word that said, "Come."**

I am personally persuaded that Jesus was thrilled when Peter asked to come to Him. I believe Jesus felt a wonderful joy when Peter actually made his way out of the boat and walked on top of the water. It so greatly grieved Jesus when Peter sank. Jesus asked, *". . . "O you of little faith, why did you doubt?""* (Matt. 14:31) Jesus actually expected for Peter to fully walk in the power and authority of God's Word, and still expects us to walk in the power of His Word today!

When Jesus declared that whoever believed in Him would do the works that He did and even greater, He meant it! Heaven expects us to walk in the supernatural, miracle-working power of the Word because from God's perspective, He's the One empowering and enabling everything He's called us to do. God expects us to do nothing He hasn't already approved and empowered us to do.

When God says we are to forgive those who have wronged us, He expects us to obey. We say we can't, but God knows better because He's the one supplying the power to do it! When we need patience with our spouses, God expects us to still serve them. When God says we should do good to those who curse us and hate us, and to pray for those who spitefully use and persecute us, He actually expects us to do just that. In other words, when the Word of God commands us to do something, we can't look at Jesus, our Lord, and say . . . "I'll think about it." To submit to the Lordship of Jesus is to submit to the Lordship and authority of His Word! They are one and the same!

As followers of Christ, we are called not just to be hearers of the Word, but to be doers. The letter of James says,

> *But be doers of the word, and not hearers only, deceiving yourselves. For if anyone is a hearer of the word and not a doer, he is like a man observing his natural face in a mirror; for he observes himself, goes away, and immediately forgets what kind of man he was. But he who looks into the perfect law of liberty and continues in it, and is not a forgetful hearer but a doer of the work, this one will be blessed in what he does.* (James 1:22–25)

If we are to experience the blessing of God, we need to not just hear the Word of God, but we must be found "doers" of the Word of God. If not, we are only deceiving ourselves to think we are actually living the life we're called to live. Following God's Word is the way to be blessed in all you do.

AT GOD'S WORD

> *When He had stopped speaking, He said to Simon, "Launch out into the deep and let down your nets for a catch." But Simon answered and said to Him, "Master, we have toiled all night and caught nothing; nevertheless, at Your word I will let down the net."* (Luke 5:4–5)

Jesus had just finished ministering to a multitude of people from Simon Peter's boat and instructed for him to go into the deep part of the sea and to let down their nets for a catch. Peter responded by telling Jesus they had already worked hard all night and that they caught nothing. *". . . Nevertheless, at Your Word I will let down the net."* (Luke 5:5).

For Peter to let down his net into the deep was an extreme act of obedience that directly went against his natural training and experience. First, fishermen know from experience that there are certain times when the fish can be caught and when they simply can't be caught. They worked all night for many hours straight, and it was just one of those times they couldn't catch anything. Second, the usual time of fishing was in the evening, not during the day. If they couldn't catch anything during the evening, then their chances of catching anything during the day were very unlikely. Peter may not have walked with Jesus very long at this point in his life, but he had a heart of obedience willing to listen and come under the authority of God's Word. He said, "Nevertheless, at Your Word I will let down the net." In other words, even though I don't think this is going to work, I will let down the net simply because You said so.

Upon Peter's obedience, they caught a great number of fish, and their net began to break (see Luke 5:6). Not only did the timing not make sense, but now the large catch didn't make sense either. The amount of fish coming to them was so great that they couldn't handle the blessing themselves. They had to call to their partners to come and help them. Now they had not one but two boats so full of fish that they both began to sink. When Peter saw it, he fell down at Jesus' knees and said, *". . . Depart from me, for I am a sinful man, O Lord!"* (Luke 5:8).

One of the great lessons of this passage is that Simon Peter was willing to come under Jesus' Word despite the fact that it didn't fit his natural understanding. He was willing to sacrifice both logic and experience and to yield himself to the leadership of God's Word!

Jesus went on to teach Simon Peter that he shouldn't be afraid, because from that point on they were going to catch men. Jesus taught His disciples powerful keys to living in the supernatural power of God. He taught them to accept and be governed by the authority of His Word even when situations seem to be hopeless. He taught them that blessing doesn't primarily flow because of human skill, luck, or human effort, but because of coming under the authority of His Word. He taught them the supernatural catch was produced by God's power, but the activation of God's blessing was released in the midst of man's obedience to God's Word. He taught them to break old expectations and get ready for new ones, because all things would be possible when following His Word!

If you look closely, some translations express that Jesus said to let down their "nets" while Peter said that he would let down his "net" singular. Jesus was telling Peter to prepare for an extremely large catch, and Peter, though he obeyed, may not have been prepared for as big of a blessing as was coming his way. God wants us to have the same vision and level of expectation as Him. He wants us to say "yes" to whatever He says and whenever He says it! He wants us to learn just as Peter did that when He speaks, when He instructs, when He commands, great things happen!

Peter didn't simply come under "a" Word or blindly follow "the" Word; He said, "At Your Word I will let down the net." It was personally linked to the fact that Jesus Himself told Peter to do it. There was a great level of honor involved in Peter's obedience that caused him to obey. Submitting ourselves under the mighty Word of God isn't just strict obedience, but should flow from both faith and honor even when God's Word fails to match our experience or understanding.

Abraham begot Isaac and offered him up as a sacrifice because He trusted God's Word and was blessed for his fear and trust in the Lord (see Gen. 22:12). It took years of labor for the enemies to build the Walls of Jericho, but they fell flat in a moment because Joshua listened to the Word of God (see Heb. 11:30)! Naaman was healed of leprosy when he dipped himself in the Jordan River at the Word of Elisha (see 2 Kings 5:14). Mary received the Word of the angel Gabriel that Jesus would be supernaturally conceived in her of the Holy Spirit and became blessed among women (see Luke 1:38).

Our Lord Jesus wants us to learn that nothing but blessing flows to us when we come under the authority of God's Word, and "let down our nets" despite the fact that it may go against our natural training and experience. Jesus wants us to be yoked to His Word so that He can produce the miraculous in our lives.

LIVING YOKED TO JESUS

Come to Me, all you who labor and are heavy laden, and I will give you rest. Take My yoke upon you and learn from Me, for I am gentle and lowly in heart, and you will find rest for your souls. For My yoke is easy and My burden is light." (Matt. 11:28–30)

The people in Jesus' day were heavily oppressed by religious legalism imposed by the scribes and Pharisees. (See Matthew 23:4.) Jesus came with an amazing invitation to come to Him and to learn from Him so they may live under the right leadership that will result in rest for their souls by receiving His grace, mercy, and forgiveness rather the harsh weight of living under legalistic burden and guilt.

The invitation Jesus gave when He said to "Take My yoke upon you and learn from Me" is so powerful. A "yoke" was a wooden frame that joined two animals, usually oxen, to pull heavy loads. One side of the yoke had a large hole, and the other side had a small hole. The larger hole was for a larger, stronger, mature ox, and the smaller hole was for a smaller, weaker, and younger ox. At first, it may appear like this mismatch of size wouldn't work, but there was a masterful purpose behind the process. The larger, more mature animal knew what to do, how to do it, and where to go. The younger animal didn't know what to do, how to do it, or where to go. When they became "yoked" together, the younger animal would be guided by the mature animal and would come to learn the right "way." When the younger animal would want to wander off and do things incorrectly, the strong animal was able to continue in the right path and the younger animal would have no choice but to follow the larger animal because they were "yoked" together. Wherever the larger animal went, the younger animal went. If the larger oxen stopped, the smaller oxen stopped. If the larger oxen moved, the smaller oxen moved. Whatever the stronger did, the weaker had to follow.

What a powerful illustration that Jesus was calling everyone to come under His Lordship and mentoring! To come under Jesus' "yoke" would mean to come under His might, strength, wisdom, power, grace, mercy, love, forgiveness, and supernatural power. Jesus invited them to get discipled and taught from Him so they may experience rest for their souls.

Still today, Jesus invites us to be "yoked" with Him so we can experience rest for our souls. The invitation has never been taken away, and all can decide to give up their own misguided ways and come under Jesus' authority. How can someone get yoked to Jesus? They get "yoked" to the Word of God.

When we're yoked to God's Word, we're yoked to Jesus! Wherever He goes, we go; whatever He speaks, we speak; whatever He prays, we pray. When we want to stray off the correct path, we'll feel the strength of His leadership keep us in the way of righteousness because we're "yoked" with Him. We fully come under His authority. If Jesus tells us to let down a net and it goes against our natural experience, then we'll let it down anyway because we're yoked to His Word!

The Bible says,

> *Forever, O Lord, Your word is settled in heaven. Your faithfulness endures to all generations; You established the earth, and it abides. They continue this day according to Your ordinances, For all are Your servants. Unless Your law had been my delight, I would then have perished in my affliction. I will never forget Your precepts, For by them You have given me life.* (Ps. 119:89–93)

To be yoked with God's Word is to be yoked to that which is settled in Heaven. It's the securest, safest place in all creation! It's the place where we're hidden from danger in the shadow of the Almighty (see Ps. 17:8) in the secret place (see Ps. 27:5).

When we grab hold of God's Word, we make the shift from natural living to supernatural living. It's at this moment the devil looks at us in the midst of his defeat and says, "Now I can't deceive them! I can't manipulate their minds; I can't pervert their hearts; I've lost my influence over them; they've hidden themselves in Christ! They've trusted God's Word!"

David said,

> *The Lord is my shepherd; I shall not want. He makes me to lie down in green pastures; He leads me beside the still waters. He restores my soul; He leads me in the paths of righteousness For His name's sake. Yea, though I walk through the valley of the shadow of death, I will fear no evil; For You are with me; Your rod and Your staff, they comfort me. You prepare a table before me in the presence of my enemies; You anoint my head with oil; My cup runs over. Surely goodness and mercy shall follow me All the days of my life; And I will dwell in the house of the Lord Forever.* (Ps. 23:1–6)

How beautiful it is to see that God's Word, Jesus, is our Shepherd and His leadership will never cause us to lack. That He makes us lie down in places of prosperity and peace. He leads us in the paths of righteousness for His name's sake, and even when we go through the most difficult of times, we need not fear anything because He's with us leading and keeping us in the right way. Thank God that He prepares a table for us in the presence of our enemies, He anoints our heads with oil, our cup runs over and goodness and mercy shall follow us all the days of our lives, and we'll dwell in the house of the Lord forever! How beautiful it is to be yoked to Jesus and His Word!

ABIDING IN JESUS

"I am the vine, you are the branches. He who abides in Me, and I in him, bears much fruit; for without Me you can do nothing. (John 15:5)

When we make the shift to live by God's Word, we need to bring how we think, speak, and act into alignment with it. This means we need to move into and develop mastery in the realm of **faith**, **prayer**, and **action**. The only way that will be possible is if we daily abide in God's Word!

We live in a generation where it's common for people to think they can produce good and holy things without the Word of God. We try to worship God without the Word, we try to pray without the Word, we try to get people delivered from bondage without the Word, etc. We're too used to making "fig leaves" and causing ourselves to become fatigued and fruitless. Jesus has taught us that we must abide in Him because without Him we can nothing.

Every Christian-related activity that becomes disconnected from God's Word becomes powerless and filled with nothing but the old nature of our flesh. Things may appear spiritual, but they aren't. They may appear holy, but they aren't. It's just natural human activity dressed up to look holy. Our devotion, worship, prayer, and every other thing we do in Christ must be found "in Christ" and in His Word.

Thus, a person who will release the Word of God in their lives is going to be a person who spends a great deal of time reading, meditating, and studying God's Word. They will move beyond a brief devotional in the morning, or the Pastor's once-a-week message, and they'll begin to "abide," or dwell, in God's Word! They will choose it as a lifestyle, and like David, they will hide God's Word within them in such a way that it will keep them in God's will. (See Psalm 119:11.) They will daily feast on the Bread of Life so every area of their lives will be filled with wisdom and power. They will become so full of God's Word that they will no longer see life circumstances through their own eyes, but will see life through the eyes of God Himself! It will no longer be them who live, but God's Word who lives in them! (See Galatians 2:20.)

BELIEVING YOUR MIRACLE

By faith we understand that the worlds were framed by the word of God, so that the things which are seen were not made of things which are visible. (Heb. 11:3)

By faith we understand that the worlds were framed by the Word of God! It's the Word that framed them. It's the Word that produced them. To have the Word is to have that which has the power to create. It's to have the source of that which changes things.

Faith in God's Word to create is so vital to releasing the supernatural power of God, and it takes tremendous pressure off us. It's not us who need to conjure up strength or power to work the works of God or change things for the better. It's the Word of God that does it! It's the Word of God that saves, heals, and delivers!

The Roman Centurion in the Gospel of Matthew knew this when He asked Jesus to simply speak His Word and his servant would be healed (see Matt. 8:8). He knew the authority of the One behind the Words would produce the results he sought! He didn't have to do anything but have the confidence in Jesus' Word, and it produced supernatural results!

Now faith is the substance of things hoped for, the evidence of things not seen. (Heb. 11:1)

It's the confident expectation that things hoped for in the unseen realm will manifest in the seen realm! It is the state of being in complete alignment and agreement with God's Word. When we completely agree with God, we're standing as one with God, and successfully and fully walking as the image of God upon the earth!

Faith isn't a feeling or an emotion. It's a deep level of spiritual awareness of who God is and what will happen through His Word. Faith doesn't create promises, but is the thing that enables access to them! Faith causes us to become aligned to God's power and enables us to release it. Faith is so important that God reveals it's impossible to please Him without it (see Heb. 11:6), and it's a "first principle" of Christianity we need to develop and master to release the miracle power of God's Word in our lives.

Jesus said to the two blind men who were healed, "... *According to your faith let it be to you.*" (Matt. 9:29). To the paralytic who broke through the roof to get to Jesus and got healed, the Bible says, "... *When Jesus saw their faith* ..." (Matt. 9:2). To the woman who touched Jesus and was healed from her flow of blood, Jesus said, "Be of good cheer, daughter; your faith has made you well." To the lepers who were healed, Jesus said, "... *Arise, go your way. Your faith has made you well.*" (Luke 17:19).

Faith accesses God's power, and it comes as we hear and abide in God's Word! Faith refuses to accept the present facts as truth! Facts are received because of education and experience. Faith is received from the release of revelation. The Bible says,

> *looking unto Jesus, the author and finisher of our faith, who for the joy that was set before Him endured the cross, despising the shame, and has sat down at the right hand of the throne of God.* (Heb. 12:2)

We need to look to Jesus! He's the author and finisher of our faith! As we focus upon Him and His Word, faith wells up inside of us to the point that it gets released and lays hold of the things it has declared! Faith is God's way, and He's taught us that faith enables us, like Peter, to walk on water, but fear and doubt cause us to sink under the present circumstances of stormy weather.

FRAMING YOUR MIRACLE

If you abide in Me, and My words abide in you, you will ask what you desire, and it shall be done for you. (John 15:7)

This is the promise of God Almighty: If we abide in Him and His Words abide in us, we can pray and ask what we desire and it shall be done! When we abide in Jesus and His Words abide in us, we become filled with Him and His will. Our will becomes His will, bringing us into perfect unity with the Father. When this level of alignment emerges, the prayers that come forth are not representative of just an individual's will but representative of God's will. When we pray for things in alignment with God's will, we know for sure that we will have what we ask! In fact, a person so filled with God's Word will find that it isn't even their words that fill their prayer, but the Words of God that fill their mouth and release God's will upon the earth. John's first letter says,

Now this is the confidence that we have in Him, that if we ask anything according to His will, He hears us. And if we know that He hears us, whatever we ask, we know that we have the petitions that we have asked of Him. (1 John 5:14–15)

We spoke about the reality that God's Word has both potential and kinetic energy in Chapter 4. It can exist dormant, and it can be released with power. Prayer is the key catalyst that moves

God's Word from its potential to its kinetic power! It literally puts God's will into motion.

As God released His pre-existent Word by speaking it into His creation, so we are called to do the same exact thing! We are to speak God's Word aloud into people's hearts, lives, bodies, and circumstances all around us! When God said, "Let there be light," there was light. It wasn't until He spoke it that His light invaded darkness. It isn't until we pray God's Word that the same thing will happen.

I've met many people who pray with only their minds. Although there is certainly a place for quiet meditation, Jesus explicitly teaches that we should do what He does and that's to speak the Word of God! Our hearts are to be filled with the Word of God, and our mouths are to release it into the atmosphere!

One day Jesus and His disciples were walking and Jesus came to a fig tree that had no fruit. Jesus spoke to the tree, and it immediately withered (see Matt. 21:19). The disciples were in shock and wondered how the tree could wither so quickly (see Matt. 21:20). Jesus then said something amazing,

> . . . *"Assuredly, I say to you, if you have faith and do not doubt, you will not only do what was done to the fig tree, but also if you say to this mountain, 'Be removed and be cast into the sea,' it will be done. And whatever things you ask in prayer, believing, you will receive."* (Matt. 21:21–22)

First we have to step back and realize that Jesus spoke to His creation. He spoke to the fig tree, He rebuked the wind and told the sea to be peaceful and still (see Mark 4:39), and He spoke to body parts such as in Mark 7:33, when Jesus told a man's ears to open. He even spoke to Lazarus' dead body commanding it to come forth in John 11:43! When Jesus spoke, He released His authority and power to specific things at specific times. If Jesus didn't specifically say Lazarus' name when He commanded him to come forth, every dead body on earth would've been raised from the dead and come out of their graves! God's creation is under the power and authority of the sound of His Word. Jesus even spoke the written form of the Word of God to overcome the devil's temptations in the wilderness. Whatever the form of God's Word may be, the power of it is released when it's spoken!

SOUND FROM HEAVEN

The Word of God is a supernatural sound, and all creation bows to it. When God released the sound of His Word into creation in the book of Genesis and said, "Let there be light," the sound of His Word and the light of His Word were one. In other words, sound and light are actually the same in many ways.

The human eye can see a certain spectrum of light and hear a certain spectrum of sound. However, there are many light forms and sound waves we can't perceive, because they're outside our natural ability to perceive. Nevertheless, they exist. The amazing reality is that science has discovered that both sound and light are both made of waves of energy but move at different speeds and algorithms. In other words, the sound of God's Word and the light of God are one. When we release the sound of God's Word, we simultaneously release God's supernatural light.

If God's Word created everything (see Heb. 11:3), then it makes perfect sense we need to release God's Word through prayer, confession, declaration, and worship because it releases the supernatural power of God!

Many times before a Sunday morning service or conference meeting begins, the people initially enter with the weight of their problems and challenges upon their shoulders. They feel beat up and sometimes overwhelmed. However, when the sound of worship is released, the atmosphere becomes Heavenly. Then, the Word of God is preached, and the countenance of the people dramatically changes. Next, we pray for the people declaring the Word of God aloud. Sickness, disease, and oppression hear the promises of God spoken, and they flee in the authority of the Name of Jesus! Truly God's Kingdom comes where His Word is released with faith!

The sound of God's Word releases the heart of God behind that Word. The sound of God's Word releases the power of God behind that Word, and the sound of God's Word releases the authority of God behind that Word!

I once saw an amazing video of a science experiment in which sand was randomly shaken on a black, flat surface. Different sound frequencies were then played in the form of high and deep tones. Amazingly, as the frequency of the sound changed, the sand automatically responded to the sound by forming beautiful and complex geometric shapes with no human intervention other than playing the different tones. The sand responded to natural sound.

When we pray for the sick aloud and command tumors to leave because we have been healed by the stripes of Jesus Christ (see Isa. 53:4–5), our faith causes our mouths to release God's Word. That evil tumor hears God's Word and flees! The fleeing tumors and sicknesses don't disappear because they listened to a human being, but they listened to God's Word in a human being! You too can speak the Word of God in faith and watch God's miracle power work in your own life!

RELEASING CREATIVE POWER

Some people are hesitant to speak God's Word with such authority, because they feel it may be too presumptuous because they are not God. These thoughts are completely understandable, but they don't agree the teachings of Jesus Christ!

God sent Jesus Christ to the earth as the first fruit example of what a sinless man would look like. Jesus walked in the likeness of man to actually model and demonstrate what we should look like after being born again! This is why Jesus quoted the Word of God when resisting the devil's temptations. He was showing us what to do! This is why Jesus spoke to the fig tree and then told His disciples that they could not only do the same but that they would do even greater. They could speak to the mountains and they would obey them. (See Matthew 21:21) Not only are we supposed to speak God's Word with authority, but we are called to do it.

When the apostle Peter saw a lame man begging for money, Peter boldly said,

> . . . *"Look at us." So he gave them his attention, expecting to receive something from them. Then Peter said, "Silver and gold I do not have, but what I do have I give you: In the name of Jesus Christ of Nazareth, rise up and walk." And he took him by the right hand and lifted him up, and immediately his feet and ankle bones received strength. So he, leaping up, stood and walked and entered the temple with them—walking, leaping, and praising God. And all the people saw him walking and praising God.* (Acts 3:4–9)

Peter spoke like Jesus in the authority of Jesus and worked a miracle of God! The people who saw and heard the apostles preach and pray even confused them with being Gods.

> *And in Lystra a certain man without strength in his feet was sitting, a cripple from his mother's womb, who had never walked. This man heard Paul speaking. Paul, observing him intently and seeing that he had faith to be healed, said with a loud voice, "Stand up straight on your feet!" And he leaped and walked. Now when the people saw what Paul had done, they raised their voices, saying in the Lycaonian language, "The gods have come down to us in the likeness of men!"* (Acts 14:8–11)

It is God's will today that we not only do what Jesus did, but also do even greater (see John 14:12)! Of course, God doesn't want us to be confused with Greek Gods like in Acts chapter 14, but He does want the world to see the living, breathing, moving, burden-bearing, chain-breaking, sickness-destroying Savior, Jesus Christ, moving in us!

If you've been praying hard and it's been fruitless, the root is that your prayer hasn't had the right mixture of faith and God's Word! If you have faith, but lack God's Word, you won't have power. If you have God's Word, but don't have faith, you won't have power. When you have both, you will have a release of God's miracle power.

Have confidence to pray and to pray boldly! Remember that your born-again creation is made in the image of God and that its DNA is the Word of God that made everything. We are spiritually made of the "stuff" that made everything! Let's pray with boldness and release the Word of God over our lives, marriages, families, finances, schools, work places, cities, countries, and world.

NEVER GIVE UP

Then He spoke a parable to them, that men always ought to pray and not lose heart, (Luke 18:1)

Anyone who's tried to live by the Word of God and release its supernatural power understands there are times that are easy and times that are a lot more challenging. Sometimes breakthrough comes quickly, and sometimes it comes slowly.

When a person prays and they seemingly do not "see" the result of their prayer, they often will get discouraged. They may say, "I tried, but it didn't work" or "I failed." We should never say such things because the Word of God always works, and we only fail if we give up and turn away from it.

Jesus spoke a parable about a widow who persistently brought her cause to an unjust judge. It took time, but her persistence paid off and even the unjust judge granted her request. The Bible says,

> *Then the Lord said, "Hear what the unjust judge said. And shall God not avenge His own elect who cry out day and night to Him, though He bears long with them? I tell you that He will avenge them speedily. Nevertheless, when the Son of Man comes, will He really find faith on the earth?"* (Luke 18:6–8)

No matter what, never give up or give in. It may be hard, and it may press your faith to the limits, but never surrender, never retreat. Decide to persist in prayer, and hold God's Word until you receive the breakthrough!

Be a person of faith and refuse to become double-minded! Stand strong on God's Word until the end, and you will overcome!

My brethren, count it all joy when you fall into various trials, knowing that the testing of your faith produces patience. But let patience have its perfect work, that you may be perfect and complete, lacking nothing. If any of you lacks wisdom, let him ask of God, who gives to all liberally and without reproach, and it will be given to him. But let him ask in faith, with no doubting, for he who doubts is like a wave of the sea driven and tossed by the wind. For let not that man suppose that he will receive anything from the Lord; he is a double-minded man, unstable in all his ways. (James 1:2–8)

THE TESTIMONY OF THE LIVING WORD

I recently traveled through the country of Madagascar in Africa ministering in three of their largest cities. It was a beautiful trip, and the people of Madagascar were in a word . . . beautiful. It's a unique people with a unique culture with unique music, food, dance, language, and manner of life. There's a great level of poverty throughout the country, and much of the population lives in need for the basics of life. The amount of suffering in the country would touch the hardest of hearts seeing many poor, sick, and suffering. I remember visiting a poor hospital and holding back rivers of tears as I saw the horrendous condition the people were in. It was inevitable for me to ponder the horrible effects of the law of sin and death as I was witnessed their pain.

When I asked pastors and Christian leaders in the country what they believed were some of the greatest spiritual challenges in the country, a common answer emerged. They all shared, "the religion of men." They explained that the people of Madagascar had heard about Jesus and they heard about the traditions of the church, but many did not have the opportunity to encounter the power of God. Thus, multitudes of poor people sat in the streets while church services were going on, and they had no apparent interest in pursuing prayer or the Word of God. They had grown so accustomed to their condition; it's as if they resolved to their reality and lacked even the awareness of hope that things could change.

Fortunately, the ministry our team partnered with not only believes in signs and wonders and the power of God's Word, but also releases them. Our team participated in a crusade in the capital city so we could release the Kingdom of power through the preaching of the Word of power.

During the crusade, the ministers and I boldly declared the Word of God. We declared the reality that Jesus and His Word are more than they've known. If they would receive Jesus and His Word, they would receive miracles! They would receive miracles from the hand of the carpenter! It was fascinating to see hope emerge on their faces as they heard about the promises of God. We were ready to speak the Word of God and release God's power!

During our time of prayer, I went to a mom and her small child. I didn't have my translator with me so I wasn't able to find out exactly what was wrong with her child. The mother motioned there was something wrong with her child's foot. I bent down to pray and commanded their foot to be healed in the Name of Jesus Christ according to the Word that was preached. The child's mother couldn't understand my English prayer as she only spoke Malagasy, one of the national languages of Madagascar. I knew that didn't matter at all because all creation hears and responds to God's Word no matter the language. The sound of God's Word and the power of God's Word are discerned by every spirit of sickness and disease and must bow to its supreme authority.

After a brief time of prayer, I took the child's hand to walk, and we walked together with no problem! Both mother and child were taken on top of the platform and testified in front of everyone! The people were able to see that miracle as well as many others, and came to know the Word of God was more than just tradition from men. They were able to see that the Son of God was alive and well and that His Word was not from men but from Heaven! They knew mere men could not produce the miracles that took place, and they gave glory to God recognizing His Word was alive and well!

This is the testimony all the world needs. Yes, there are very large and powerful ministries preaching the Word of God in many nations with signs and wonders, but God desires for that power to be in your home, your marriage, your job, your mind, your emotions, and your whole life! He desires for a new hunger to emerge in our lives for the supernatural, miracle-working power of God's Word!

God commands all believers to take the Word of Life (see Phil. 2:16) and the Word of power and release it everywhere to everyone! God's Word commands us to go into the world and not only preach, but manifest the power of His Word by healing the sick, cleansing the lepers, and raising the dead! God wants His Word to be manifested so it may be received properly, because when we receive God's living Word for what it truly is, we become temples of His Word and carriers of the authority of the Kingdom of Heaven! To receive the testimony of the Word of God is to receive the testimony of Jesus, and this is what enables us to release the supernatural power of God's Word!

CHAPTER SUMMARY POINTS

1. To live by the Word of God is to live by that which made the Heavens and all who dwell in them. It's the highest level of living, and there's no greater authority in all creation other than God's Holy Word! All things are under its authority, and we should come into the presence of God with awe that "He spoke, and it was done; He commanded, and it stood fast."

2. We should realize, however, that to truly live according to the principles, teachings, and instructions of the Word of God presents us with a significant shift in how most usually live.

3. One of the simplest but profound things to learn is that Heaven actually expects us to follow God's Word.

4. Simon Peter was willing to come under the Word of Jesus despite the fact that it didn't fit his natural understanding. He was willing to sacrifice both logic and experience and to yield himself to the leadership of God's Word!

5. When we're yoked to Jesus, we're yoked to the Word of God! Wherever He goes, we go; whatever He speaks, we speak; whatever He prays, we pray. When we want to stray off the correct path, we'll feel the strength of His leadership correctly lead us because we're "yoked" with Him. We will fully come under His authority. If Jesus tells us to let down a net and it goes against our natural experience, then we'll let it down.

6. The person who will release the Word of God in their lives is going to be a person who spends a great deal of time reading, meditating, and studying God's Word.

7. It's not us who need to conjure up strength or power to work the works of God or change things for the better. It's the

Word of God that does it! It's the Word of God that saves, heals, and delivers!

8. Prayer is the key catalyst that moves God's Word from its potential to its kinetic power! It literally puts God's will into motion.

9. The sound of God's Word releases the heart of God behind that Word. The sound of God's Word releases the power of God behind that Word, and the sound of God's Word releases the authority of God behind that Word!

10. It is God's will today that we not only do what Jesus did, but also do even greater today!

11. When a person prays and they seemingly does not "see" the result of their prayer, they often will get discouraged. They may say, "I tried, but it didn't work" or "I failed." We should never say such things because the Word of God always works, and we only fail if we give up and turn away from God's Word.

QUESTIONS FOR REFLECTION

1. What changes do you need to make in your faith-life to successfully shift from relying on natural wisdom to God's wisdom in His Word?

2. Are you willing to "let down your nets" when God's Word may conflict with your experience?

3. What improvements can you make to abide in Jesus and His Word?

4. What specific things do you need to begin speaking the Word of God to in your life? What promises of God will you speak?

PRAYER

Father, I'm willing to make the shift from living in my strength to living in Your strength. Help me to lay down my wisdom, my logic, and my experience so I can live at the level of blessing provided by Your Word. Train me to think what You think, see what You see, and hear what You hear. Grant me boldness to speak Your Word in prayer to the things in my life and the life of others. I declare that I will never give up and I won't turn back. I put my trust in You and Your Word. I ask this in the Name of Jesus Christ! Amen!

Chapter 12

DIVINE BLUEPRINT

GOD'S CALL TO INTIMACY

Now there was leaning on Jesus' bosom one of His disciples, whom Jesus loved. (John 13:23)

I've always thought about this picture of John leaning on Jesus' chest. It's such a beautiful picture of intimacy with the Son of God. The thing I love is that John was so close to Jesus' chest that he was able to hear the heartbeat of God Himself. Jesus was so much more to John than theology, doctrine, or tradition. John was so close to Jesus and experienced his love in such a powerful way.

I'm persuaded that God loves you, and I, with this same love, and desires for us to lay our head upon Jesus' bosom and to experience His heartbeat just like John. Our Father sent Jesus to adopt us and fill us with His Holy Spirit, and awaits our homecoming to Him in Heaven at his appointed hour.

Our destiny is to spend eternity with our Father and His Son, Jesus, in Heaven! We are destined to behold the beauty of God and aspects of His creation we've never even dreamed of. Truly . . .

> *"Eye has not seen, nor ear heard, Nor have entered into the heart of man The things which God has prepared for those who love Him."* (1 Cor. 2:9)

Until our time comes to pass from this life to the next, our Father desires for us to experience an intimacy with Him far greater than we've ever dreamed of. He desires to manifest Himself to us through dreams, visions, signs, and wonders, but still chooses to primarily reveal Himself through His Holy Word! He desires for His Word to be planted deeply in our lives so its glory will not only be personally experienced in our lives, but also in the lives of those around us.

GOD'S CALL TO WITNESS

> *And I fell at his feet to worship him. But he said to me, "See that you do not do that! I am your fellow servant, and of your brethren who have the testimony of Jesus. Worship God! For the testimony of Jesus is the spirit of prophecy."* (Rev. 19:10)

There's an entire world around us desperately in need of relief from their fear, pain, and torment. As Christians, we've often fallen short of being the witnesses of Jesus Christ God has called us to be. In addition, many churches have fallen short of providing the proper example of what Christianity truly is and how powerful the Word of God is upon the earth. In many ways, the collective witness of God's people has discouraged the lost from reading the Bible and seeking a church.

The reality is that the majority of people who are headed to hell in their sin may never be inspired to interact with God's Word, until they interact with a true witness of the power of His Word. Someone who not only preaches the Word, but also lives by it. Someone who not only lives by it, but also demonstrates its power in daily life. The world is crying out to be healed and saved from their destructions, and we need to be living witnesses and ministers of the Word God has sent to accomplish it! (See Psalm 107:20.)

Our Father is a good Father who longs to call every sinner into His presence through His Son, Jesus. He hears the cries of the hurting, the hungry, and the homeless. His eyes aren't interested in seeing big buildings, marble floors, or fancy multimedia equipment. God said through the prophet Isaiah,

Thus says the Lord: "Heaven is My throne, And earth is My footstool. Where is the house that you will build Me? And where is the place of My rest? For all those things My hand has made, And all those things exist," Says the Lord. "But on this one will I look: On him who is poor and of a contrite spirit, And who trembles at My word. (Isa. 66:1–2)

He's interested in seeing a people who will tremble at His Word! Many read, study, and preach God's Word, but the Father is looking for those who will tremble at His Word. Such a level of honor, humility, submission, and fear of the Lord will cause us not only to know God's Word, but also to become one with God's Word so we may be the witnesses God is calling us to be. The witnesses we need to be for our families, our friends, and our enemies to be saved.

This is what's required to bring about the worldwide tsunami of glory the Father desires to release. This is what's required to fill the earth with the testimony of Jesus Christ upon the earth! God desires to see the victory of His Son's death, burial, and resurrection being received and applied to the lives of the young and old, the rich and the poor, and everyone in between.

All must have the opportunity to see that Jesus is alive and reigns forever more! All must get the opportunity to see Jesus as He truly is, fall at His feet at the foot of the cross, and lay down their burdens of sin and shame. All must have the opportunity to receive the righteousness of Christ and the rest that comes from receiving Him as Lord. All must have the chance to get delivered from their sickness and disease, and live in the peace and joy of God's love. All must get the chance to receive and live with the testimony of Jesus.

So let us fully yield ourselves to the plan of God our Father to receive the supernatural nature of His Word, to access it with unshakable faith, and to release its miracle-working power so we may be faithful ambassadors of His Word, Unleashing Heaven's Breath.

> *And Jesus came and spoke to them, saying, "All authority has been given to Me in Heaven and on earth. Go therefore and make disciples of all the nations, baptizing them in the name of the Father and of the Son and of the Holy Spirit, teaching them to observe all things that I have commanded you; and lo, I am with you always, even to the end of the age." Amen.* (Matt. 28:18–20)

ABOUT THE AUTHOR

As the founding Pastor of Abundant Grace Christian Church and Jesus Reigns International, Inc., located in Rutherford, NJ, Pastor Steve Hannett has a heart to see God's apostolic vision through Jesus Christ fulfilled in every way.

He carries a powerful apostolic, teaching, and healing anointing and travels domestically and internationally preaching, teaching, and advancing the Kingdom of God with signs, wonders, and miracles through the working of God's Holy Spirit.

The Lord uses Pastor Steve to bring the Gospel's promise of healing to many through worship, teaching, and prayer. His testimony of being healed from cancer has been featured by such ministries as TBN America, TBN Africa, Breath of Life Missions, Alerta television, and many others.

He serves as a Local Faculty member of the Antioch School of Church Planting and Leadership Development and as a Certified Partner of BILD International helping churches to develop and implement church-based Theological Training programs both domestically and internationally. Pastor Steve also serves on the Apostolic Leadership Council of Christ Covenant Coalition, a growing church network rooted in the tradition of Christ and

His Apostles. In addition, he serves on the Board of Jesus to Muslims, a ministry dedicated to reaching Muslims for Christ.

He is the blessed husband of his beautiful wife, Kate Hannett, and has three wonderful children.